MMA NOW!

BRIAN SOBIE &
ADAM ELLIOTT SEGAL

MMA NOW!

THE STARS AND STORIES OF MIXED MARTIAL ARTS

FIREFLY BOOKS

A FIREFLY BOOK

Published by Firefly Books Ltd. 2014

First printing

Publisher Cataloging-in-Publication Data (U.S.)
A CIP record for MMA Now!/978-1-77085-291-4 is available from
the Library of Congress

Library and Archives Canada Cataloguing in Publication
A CIP record for MMA Now!/978-1-77085-291-4 is available from
Library and Archives Canada

Published in the United States by
Firefly Books (U.S.) Inc.
P.O. Box 1338, Ellicott Station
Buffalo, New York 14205

Published in Canada by
Firefly Books Ltd.
50 Staples Avenue, Unit 1
Richmond Hill, Ontario L4B 0A7

Cover and interior design: Matt Filion
Creative direction and editing: Steve Cameron

Printed in the United States of America

The publisher gratefully acknowledges the financial support for our publishing program
by the Government of Canada through the Canada Book Fund as administered by the
Department of Canadian Heritage.

Captions
Page 2: Welterweight Jon Fitch attempts to secure an armbar submission against Erick Silva
at UFC 153 in Rio de Janeiro, Brazil.

Page 5: UFC Octagon Girl Brittney Palmer signals the start of the first round between Kajan
Johnson and Tae Hyun Bang during UFC 174 in Vancouver, Canada.

Page 6: Ryan Bader takes down Rafael Cavalcante during UFC 174. Bader won a three-round
unanimous decision.

CONTENTS

INTRODUCTION

MIXED MARTIAL ARTS has come a long way. From fringe activity to one of the fastest-growing sports on earth, MMA is now in its golden age. It's truly an exciting time to be a fight fan!

Combat sports have been around as long as men have been standing. As UFC president Dana White told the Vancouver Board of Trade prior to UFC 174, "Before a guy threw a ball in a hoop, a guy hit a puck with a stick, or hit a ball over a wall . . . two men were put on this earth, somebody threw a punch and whoever [else] was standing around ran over and watched. Fighting is the first sport ever, and will be the last sport ever."

Fighting is simply in our DNA, White concluded. And of course, he's right. Over the course of history, a variety of fighting disciplines, like judo, vale tudo, karate, sambo, boxing, wrestling and jiu-jitsu, have emerged, and what we call MMA is a hybrid of all of these.

Since jiu-jitsu master Royce Gracie captured the belt at UFC 1 in 1993 — a tournament-style event with no weight classes — it's been a long and winding road for the once-fledgling sport. But despite the myriad controversies, lost dollars, countless beefs, rule changes and revolving door of promotions over the last two decades — such as Pride, Pancrase, Strikeforce and the UFC — MMA has found a way to not only survive but to also thrive. Women's MMA is now on the rise, and the UFC is expanding across the globe, hosting fights in Turkey, Ireland and New Zealand. New weight classes, including flyweight and strawweight, have been added in recent years, and top fighters come from far-flung destinations such as Dagestan, Sweden and Iceland. The UFC is no longer confined to pay-per-view television, either. Fans from across the world can now watch cards on cable or download fights directly to their phones or laptops.

Any successful sport needs its idols, those personalities that rise above the fray to become icons. From Gracie to Ken Shamrock to Chuck Liddell to Georges St-Pierre, the

UFC has successfully manufactured star after star. And while Georges St-Pierre's seven-year reign as the UFC's welterweight champion has come to an end (as all title reigns must), there is no doubt his work in the ring along with his clean-cut persona helped usher in a new era of MMA, one that bridged the gap toward mainstream acceptance. Although GSP may be semi-retired since his last fight versus Johny Hendricks — and recovering from another devastating knee injury suffered in training — we haven't yet seen the last of him in the octagon.

But the torch has officially been passed, and fighters like Jon Jones, Rory MacDonald and Anthony Pettis are becoming marquee names in their own right. That's not to disrespect the legends who paved the way for these current stars. We hope you'll find the stories of Japanese trailblazers like Kazushi Sakuraba and Masakatsu Funaki compelling; we hope you'll see echoes of your favorite UFC fighters in the stories of Liddell, Randy Couture and Fedor Emelianenko. Perhaps you'll discover a new favorite in our rising stars section or learn a thing or two about the early days of MMA.

The UFC may be big business now, but don't let that overshadow why we watch — when two fighters go toe to toe, anything can happen. Dan Henderson versus Mauricio "Shogun" Rua at UFC 139 is a perfect example, as the two aging light heavyweights slugged it out for five unbelievable rounds in a fight for the ages that few anticipated. Even more exciting was Lyoto Machida's Karate Kid-style front kick to the head that ended the night of former UFC champion Randy Couture at UFC 129. And more recently, the unheralded T.J. Dillashaw absolutely dismantled UFC champion Renan Barao (who hadn't lost in nearly a decade) for the bantamweight belt at UFC 173. These stories are why we watch: for jaw-dropping moments and unpredictable endings.

So whether you're a hardcore fan or a newbie, we hope you'll be as excited as we are for the new era of mixed martial arts.

It's time . . .

– Brian Sobie and Adam Elliott Segal

Dan Severn and Ken Shamrock grapple during their bout at UFC 6 in 1995. Shamrock defeated Severn with a guillotine choke at 2:14 of the first round.

A view of the octagon and crowd at UFC 83 in Montreal, Canada. Native son Georges St-Pierre defeated Matt Serra for the UFC welterweight title.

A BRIEF HISTORY OF MMA

IT HAD BEEN a long night for the more than 20,000 fans who squeezed themselves into Montreal's Bell Centre on March 16, 2013. They had been patiently sitting through preliminary battles, enjoying the action and eagerly awaiting the main event of UFC 158: the mixed martial arts battle between Georges St-Pierre and Nick Diaz. The matchup had been talked about and promised for so long, the fans teased for years — and it was now about to happen. The first fighter to enter the octagon was Diaz, and as he stood waiting for St-Pierre, the crowd buzzed in anticipation of the arrival of the man UFC president Dana White once called "the most famous athlete ever to come out of Canada."

The event turned out to be no less popular than the charismatic St-Pierre himself. UFC 158, a win for GSP, generated $3.7 million from the live gate and nearly $50 million from the 800,000 people who purchased the show on pay-per-view. It was another fiscal knockout for Zuffa Entertainment, the parent company of the Ultimate Fighting Championship, or UFC. The fight's success was due largely to the popularity of St-Pierre and the swagger of Diaz, who engendered a love–hate relationship from UFC fans. Either way, the pairing was good for business, and UFC 158 is a prime example of how Zuffa is at the apex of the fighting world, generating billions of dollars a year and establishing a significant presence around the world.

But it wasn't always this way. Mixed martial arts has fought a long, uphill battle for mainstream acceptance, and although the focus of this book is largely on today's top fighters, it is important to understand the history of MMA so that current events and athletes can be examined within the context of a sport that is well over 2,000 years old.

★★★

THERE HAS LONG been a fascination with the violent spectacle of two willing opponents engaged in hand-to-hand combat. Some enjoy the purity and simplicity of the sport, the same way the Olympic 100-meter dash establishes who, at that moment in time, is the fastest man on the planet. In this way, the fighting that mixed martial arts (and the UFC) offers showcases the best all-around fighters in the world (in their given weight classes, of course). Thousands of years ago it was this sort of contest that decided tribal leaders or who would have access to the best food or most attractive mates. The need to know who is physically superior to whom is a very base and pure desire that produces a hardwired, universal guttural reaction — both positive and negative — in all of us. And staged fights that play off of this desire have seemingly been around as long as we have.

The first mention of fighting as sport is a literary one and goes back to Greek mythology, where it's said that Heracles and Theseus used a combination of boxing and wrestling to confront their opponents. It is generally accepted that the first documented competition that bears a resemblance to modern mixed martial arts was called

pankration and was introduced by the ancient Greeks at the Olympic Games of 648 BC. The word *pankration* can be translated as "all strength," *pan* meaning all and *kratos* meaning strength. Later, the Romans adopted pankration into their sporting festivals until it was eventually abolished, along with gladiatorial contests and pagan rituals, by Christian Byzantine emperor Theodosius I in 393 AD. This would not be the last time a civic leader would make it problematic to stage fights.

It was 1,500 years later in 1896 when Frenchman Pierre de Coubertin resurrected the Olympic Games and all its ancient sports. De Coubertin, however chose to omit pankration from the list of Olympic contests after the influential Archbishop of Lyon publicly spoke against the inclusion of such fighting.

And so the modern Olympics went ahead with only two combat-type sports: fencing and wrestling. Boxing was added to the slate of events in 1904, and judo made its first appearance in 1964. Boxing, though, was the combat sport that most captivated audiences in Europe and North America — and for a long time it was the fighting sport that people believed determined the might of men.

With pankration decidedly left behind, the next events that could be considered legitimate mixed martial arts bouts were held in Brazil in the 1950s. These were called vale tudo, meaning "anything goes" or "no rules," and although they did have some rules, they were often brutal contests that were traditionally part of the Brazilian underground fight scene. The exception to this was a series of highly publicized vale tudo fights between jiu-jitsu legend Helio Gracie and his protégé Valdemar Santana, as well as a second series of fights between Santana and Grace's nephew Carlson Gracie.

The bouts were big news in Brazil among those in the jiu-jitsu community, but with little fanfare in the

Left: Georges St-Pierre celebrates with a young fan after defending his welterweight title against Nick Diaz at UFC 158.
Right: A poster for boxing at the 1924 Olympics in Paris, France.

mainstream media to spread the details of the events to a larger audience, they were largely unheard of in the rest of the world. As for the two combatants, Santana's name would live on as an early adopter of mixed martial arts, while Helio Gracie's reputation as a fighter would later be enhanced by his progeny, many of whom became historically significant mixed martial artists.

Mixed martial arts as we know it today didn't pick up any real momentum until the early 1990s. However, the notion of pitting two of the world's best combatants (of separate disciplines) against each other came together in an awkward night in 1976. The fight in question pitted pro wrestler

Boxer Muhammad Ali tries to dodge a kick from wrestler Antonio Inoki during their much-maligned fight in 1976.

Antonio Inoki against world-class boxer Muhammad Ali.

Despite competing almost exclusively in worked matches (scripted fighting with predetermined endings), Inoki was seen by the Japanese public as a real threat to the great boxer. On Ali's part, his camp thought the event was only an exhibition. But after a visit to Inoki's training gym proved the large wrestler was preparing for a real fight, Ali threatened to pull out of the event unless rule changes were made. In the end, Inoki was not allowed to throw or tackle Ali, and he couldn't even kick him unless he had one knee on the ground. The rule changes turned the fight into a farce, with Inoki scooting around on his backside in crab-like fashion trying to kick Ali, who did his best to keep out of the wrestler's way and throw the

odd punch. Although the fight made a lot of money and the two men became lifelong friends, the event itself was a joke and a low point in Ali's career.

Inoki's popularity as a pro wrestler in Japan was due in part to his ability to make his fights look real, skills he learned from Belgian professional wrestler Karl Gotch. Gotch, who was born Karl Charles Istaz, had a large but often forgotten impact on mixed martial arts. As a professional wrestler he was never very popular, lacking the personality to make it in scripted wrestling. But he was considered one of the premier shooters (real fighters) in the world. Even still, it wasn't until he took his skills and knowledge to Japan that he earned the respect he deserved. His impact on Japanese pro wrestling was enormous, as he trained fighters to work as stiffs — meaning to fight in a way that seemed to be real. He also preached the art of submission and instructed his wrestlers to use real submission holds, giving them formidable expertise that translated well to real fighting.

The stiff style of pro wrestling became very popular with the Japanese public and triggered the rise of many fighting promotions. One was the Universal Wrestling Federation (UWF), which was very popular during its two years of existence from 1984 to 1986. The stars of the UWF were men like Akira Maeda, Gran Hamada and Satoru Sayama (all of whom worked with or were influenced in some way by Gotch). The promotion eventually disbanded when a stiff but worked match between Maeda and Sayama became real when Maeda started throwing real kicks. Maeda left UWF and went to the New Japan Pro-Wrestling promotion, while Sayama started an organization called Shooto, which for all intents and purposes was the first modern mixed martial arts promotion (despite the fact it did occasional scripted pro wrestling bouts).

Shooto was followed by the Japanese fighting promotion Pancrase in 1993. Started by Japanese pro wrestlers and Gotch disciples Masakatsu Funaki and Minoru Suzuki, Pancrase matches were almost all real and followed mixed martial arts rules, with the exception that closed-fisted punches to the head were illegal and submission holds had to be broken once a fighter reached the ropes. The promotion served as the launching pad for future UFC stars Ken Shamrock, Frank Shamrock, Bas Rutten and Guy Mezger, and it still operates today as one of Japan's premier MMA loops under the name Pancrase Hybrid Wrestling.

ALTHOUGH WRESTLERS had established mixed martial arts promotions in Japan and the Brazilian fight community sponsored vale tudo bouts, the rise of MMA in the United States was left to an advertiser who had a eureka moment while reading his copy of *Playboy*.

It was 1989, and Art Davie had just finished reading a fascinating *Playboy* article that featured Brazilian Rorion Gracie and his jiu-jitsu academy in California. Rorion was the son of the legendary Helio Gracie, and he had moved to Torrance, California, to teach jiu-jitsu. He built the reputation for his academy (and for jiu-jitsu) by issuing an open challenge to all comers. Essentially, Gracie offered $100,000 to anyone who could beat him in a "no-holds-barred" fight — no rules, no time limit; last man standing wins. Davie was astonished to read that no one had been able to collect the reward, and more impressive to him was that Gracie had been able to defeat all challengers without hurting them. He simply used his legendary grappling skills to force opponents to tap out, or he "put them to sleep" with a choke hold that momentarily cut off oxygen to the brain.

Davie, who trained in martial arts to keep himself in shape, had been playing with the idea of starting a martial arts contest that pitted fighters from different disciplines against one another to see which of the martial arts would ultimately prevail. The more he learned about jiu-jitsu and the Gracie family, the more he felt he'd found what he needed to turn his idea into a reality.

Davie sought out Gracie, and together they came up with what they called War of the Worlds: a tournament that would determine the world's best fighter and the most effective martial arts discipline. The two men unsuccessfully pitched their idea to a number of television executives, including those at HBO and Showtime. It wasn't until they met with Bob Meyrowitz, president of the Semaphore Entertainment Group (SEG), that they managed to generate some interest. Meyrowitz had built his name in radio and was best known for creating and producing the *King Biscuit Radio Hour*, a syndicated radio show that ran for more than 30 years. By the time Meyrowitz met with Davie and Gracie, he and SEG had built a reputation through their promotion of a number of off-beat pay-per-view events like live rock concerts and the notorious Battle of the Sexes tennis match between Billie Jean King and Bobby Riggs.

Photos from UFC 1 (clockwise from left): Champion Royce Gracie is awarded his prize money; Gracie is hoisted by his cornermen after defeating Gerard Gordeau in the final; Patrick Smith tries to ward off a kick to the stomach by Ken Shamrock.

With SEG on board, things really began to take shape. The name of the tournament was changed from War of the Worlds to Ultimate Fighting Championship. They also decided to have the combatants fight within an eight-sided cage they called the octagon to create a more dynamic visual experience and to keep fighters from saving themselves when they got in trouble by sticking their heads outside the ropes, as they did under Pancrase rules.

UFC 1 took place on November 12, 1993, and is considered the beginning of modern-day North American mixed martial arts. It was held in Denver's McNichols Arena, mainly because the state of Colorado did not have a boxing commission. Needing a boxing commission's sanctioning for the event would have doomed the Ultimate Fighting Championship, as this new sport didn't observe the most basic rules of boxing, such as weight classes or the use of specific gloves.

UFC 1 was an eight-man knockout tournament featuring world-class fighters from boxing, kickboxing, sumo wrestling, jiu-jitsu and professional wrestling. American Ken Shamrock, who had already fought in Pancrase in Japan, and Royce Gracie, a younger brother

to Rorion, were early favorites. Royce's participation, however, was somewhat of a surprise to those who were familiar with the Gracie family. Most had expected Rickson Gracie to be the Gracie of choice for this event. He was considered the toughest of the Gracies and had an unsubstantiated 400-0 record as a street fighter. Insiders assumed Royce was chosen because of an inner family feud that had been festering between Rorion and Rickson. However, the truth had far more to do with the fact that Royce was noticeably smaller and slighter than Rickson, and the visuals of the unimposing Royce defeating much larger opponents would better underscore the powers of jiu-jitsu.

It was a testament to Rorion's understanding of fighting that Royce went on to win UFC 1, 2, and 4 and is considered by many to be one of the most influential fighters in the history of the UFC. Royce's victories seemed to indicate that the Gracie brand of Brazilian jiu-jitsu was the world's most effective fighting sport. However, history has shown that to be only partially true. As mixed martial arts evolved, being better than your opponent at a certain discipline, like jiu-jitsu, was all well and good, but winning was based not so much on discipline as it was on which fighter was the most complete combatant. Most fighters today look to have a specialty in one or two disciplines while also being skillful in the defensive aspects of many others.

During the early UFC events, Royce was able to defeat kickboxers and boxers by taking them to the ground before they could inflict any serious damage on him. Once on the ground none of the standup fighters had even the most basic understanding of ground fighting and were usually submitted fairly quickly. The only opponent who gave Gracie troubles in the early UFC events was Ken Shamrock. He had been in Japan doing submission training with the Pancrase fighters since 1992 and still believes, to this day, that he would have won UFC 1 had he not made what he calls a "stupid mental mistake" against Gracie during their semifinal match.

Besides Gracie's strong performance and the introduction of jiu-jitsu to the North American public, there were other strange and memorable happenings at UFC 1 that enabled the event to permeate the consciousness of the sport-watching public. In the first bout of the evening, Dutch kickboxer Gerard Gordeau landed a kick on the massive sumo wrestler Teila Tuli, knocking his tooth flying. He followed that up with a bare-knuckled punch to Tuli's head and the fight was over. Tuli's face was a mess, and Gordeau broke a hand and foot. Despite fighting with the two painful injuries, Gordeau won his semifinal match before losing to Gracie in the final.

A crowd of 7,600 people showed up at McNichols Arena to witness UFC 1, and another 86,000 people spent $14.95 each to watch the event live on pay-per-view. The gross was an astonishing $1.2 million, which, for the time, was an amazing figure for an event with no history, no mainstream television support and a group of eight largely unknown athletes.

UFC 1 was even more significant in historical terms. It introduced a new version of the ancient sport of pankration to a wide audience, and discussions about the event went viral. The promoters had hit lightning in a bottle. UFC 2 reaped the benefits of this, and more than 300,000 people purchased the pay-per-view event. It was astonishing. In ensuing years the UFC's popularity would ebb and flow, but what remained constant was its presence in the consciousness of North American sports fans.

★ ★ ★

BY THE MID 1990s, the UFC had a problem. With the novelty of the style of fighting wearing off, and the majority of bouts being won by those fighters who understood how to submit their opponents, the UFC looked to be a one-trick pony, which was very evident at UFC 5 in 1995.

That particular event had an eight-man tournament as well as a main-card bout between Ken Shamrock and Royce Gracie that was billed as the first UFC superfight. The buy rate of 260,000 viewers was excellent, but the in-cage action was not — at least in terms of entertainment value. The Gracie vs. Shamrock bout went 36 minutes, most of which featured Shamrock simply lying on top of Gracie, while his father and chief cornerman, Bob Shamrock, shouted at his son, "Do something!" The fight was called a draw, and the disappointing finish would come to symbolize the start of the first down period for the UFC and mixed martial arts in North America.

In short, the fighters weren't evolving as quickly as the appetite for the matches was growing, and with strategically

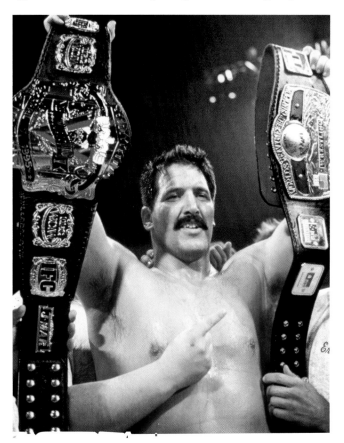

Dan Severn celebrates after winning the eight-man tournament at UFC 5 in 1995.

sound grappling and submission fighters working their way to victory, audiences were getting bored. Wrestlers, like Dan Severn and Mark Coleman, had started to win the majority of competitions by using their power, balance and leverage to neutralize their opponents' submission and striking skills. That made bouts slower and less dramatic, with many wins coming by decision after round upon round of one fighter lying on top of another, or by a series of blows that eventually did enough damage to earn a stoppage from an observant referee. Most fans relished knockout punches and kicks, or a lightning-quick submission done by an accomplished jiu-jitsu master, and were less excited by the tedium of a dominating wrestler. This was a problem for the UFC, one that needed a couple of years and a surprise champion to solve. But resolving the in-match entertainment conundrum was a small-scale issue compared with the haymaker they were about to receive from a United States senator.

Before running for president, John McCain was a popular and powerful senator who wasn't afraid to voice his opinion. In 1996, a VHS tape of a UFC event landed on his desk, and in short order he decided to make it his mission to shut down what he called "human cockfighting." He sent letters to all 50 states asking them to ban the sport. Thirty-six states complied with his request and made it illegal to hold a UFC competition within their borders. The political pressure also convinced most major pay-per-view companies to cease carrying the events as part of their service. This was a financially crippling development for SEG, as the bulk of its revenue came from pay-per-views.

In spite of the organization's financial and political woes during this time, there were some positive developments that would ultimately help propel the UFC back to prominence in the next decade. Because its reputation for violence made it a pariah to the mainstream media, no major newspapers or television networks would cover UFC events, and few would profile its fighters. Luckily for the UFC, the Internet was now a regular part of many people's lives, and that new method of information distribution gave rise to a small group of websites that provided a community for like-minded fight fans who enjoyed the UFC. Websites such as mmaweekly.com, fullcontactfighter.com and sherdog.com provided news and analysis on fights and fighters that were seldom seen elsewhere. Fan forums like The Underground gave the sport a voice and direct connection to its fans, with

fighters, managers and promoters even participating in online discussions.

And while technology and information were changing the way fans interacted with the sport, the sport began to evolve as well. It was now called mixed martial arts, and fighters studied all types of martial arts — wrestlers learned how to strike, and kickboxers mastered the basics of wrestling and jiu-jitsu so they were able to defend themselves adequately when a fight went to the ground. At UFC 14 in 1997, kickboxer Maurice Smith shocked the experts by defeating wrestler Mark Coleman by decision, despite the fact that the majority of the fight took place on the ground, where most would expect Coleman to dominate.

Smith's victory was one of the harbingers of the impending arrival of a new breed of UFC fighters. Men such as Frank Shamrock, Guy Mezger, Jens Pulver and Josh Barnett could now end fights by knocking their opponents out or by using a variety of submissions. Becoming a world-class mixed martial artist was incredibly demanding. Competitors had to be in top physical and mental condition. They often trained six to eight hours a day and forced themselves to learn four, sometimes five martial arts. The end result was the creation of a new type of athlete — competitors who were both physically and intellectually exceptional and multifaceted. They looked like lean bodybuilders, came from all over the world and were intelligent and well-spoken. In other words they were a marketer's dream.

The rules and the sanctioning bodies were evolving too. The province of Quebec in Canada developed rules and procedures for mixed martial arts and worked with the state of New Jersey to create an organized and safe environment for mixed martial arts competitions that ultimately led to the sanctioning of UFC events in that state. When UFC 28 took place in November of 2000 at the Trump Taj Mahal Resort and Casino, it became the first UFC event to be sanctioned by the New Jersey State Athletic Control Board — the second most influential group of its kind behind only the powerful Nevada State Athletic Commission.

The sanctioning victory in New Jersey could not have come at a better time for SEG, which was on the verge of bankruptcy. The sanctioning gave SEG and the UFC major credibility and hope for a return to pay-per-view across the country. All it would take was for the promotion to be accepted by the Nevada State Athletic Commission. Buoyed by the success of UFC 28, SEG head Bob Meyrowitz was ready to go to Nevada and apply, but insider information told him the votes weren't there and that the UFC would get stuffed in Nevada. Despite desperately needing the sanctioning to avoid bankruptcy, Meyrowitz decided not to take the chance on a "no" vote. Instead, he sold the UFC to Station Casinos president Lorenzo Fertitta, who just happened to be the commissioner of the Nevada State Athletic Commission, and his brother, Frank Fertitta. The $2 million purchase signalled the beginning of the UFC's return to prosperity.

IN BUSINESS, AS in life, timing is everything, and the purchase of the UFC in 2000 by the Fertitta brothers (who run the UFC under the Zuffa Entertainment label) was nearly perfect timing — in hindsight at least. When the Fertittas made their gamble, the early returns weren't promising. But with firm enough resolve to weather the storm, the brothers managed to hang on long enough for a whole group of stars to align and for their investment to start paying dividends.

At the outset of the purchase, the issues in need of immediate attention were legal — and the product would wait. Lorenzo Fertitta knew SEG had cleared a huge hurdle for him by receiving sanctioning in New Jersey. With his stature in Nevada as it was, sanctioning of the UFC by the Nevada State Athletic Commission was somewhat of a formality, and it was given shortly after Zuffa's purchase of the UFC.

The move put the UFC back on basic cable pay-per-view. It was another quick victory but one that certainly did not guarantee instant profits — quite the opposite in fact. The UFC was no longer the novelty it was in 1993, and most of the big names of the early days were no longer competing. Without the star power of fighters like Royce Gracie and Ken Shamrock, the pay-per-view operators demanded that Zuffa guarantee a buy-rate number. So, if that number

was 150,000 buys at $40 each and only 100,000 pay-per-views were sold, then the UFC would have to make up the difference of 50,000 buys, or $2 million. It was a dangerous scenario, and Zuffa paid the price in their first year back on pay-per-view, losing an estimated $10 million in their first 18 months of operation.

Fortunately for UFC fans, the Fertittas had the resources and business vision to withstand these types of losses far longer than the typical investor. Both brothers were on the list of the 500 wealthiest men in the world. They had taken over and grown the Station Casinos business started by their father, Frank Jr., and added real estate holdings, a beer company and various other ventures. In addition to their business experience, they were also relatively young when they bought the UFC, with Frank in his early 40s

UFC co-owners, Lorenzo (left) and Frank Fertitta, attend UFC on Fox 1 on November 12, 2011.

and Lorenzo in his late 30s. They both understood their market — males 18 to 35 — and believed in the power of the Internet to help reach their audience. The Fertittas, along with Dana White, quickly and aggressively created an online identity in the early 2000s and endorsed their product widely on the sites where fight fans congregated. It was a strategy that would pay off for the company — just not for another five or six years.

Even with a strong web presence, the Fertittas weren't dummies, and they knew they needed regular television exposure if the promotion was really going to make it. The promotion's most notable foray into television at this time was the inclusion of UFC 37.5 on Fox Sportsnet's *The Best Damn Sports Show* in June 2002. Ratings for the show were never made public, but they were only good enough to warrant the airing of just two more UFC events on the station. But the real breakthrough was about to come.

The Ultimate Fighter is a reality TV show that features 16 fighters living in one house under the tutelage of two established UFC fighters. Each week, a fight is staged and the losing fighter is eliminated from the competition. The final two combatants fight for a chance at a UFC contract. Launched in 2005 as a last-ditch attempt to salvage the promotion, *The Ultimate Fighter* can now arguably be called the most important development in the history of the UFC. In historical terms the show rests alongside the *Gillette Cavalcade of Sports* (boxing) and *Monday Night Football* as television shows that changed the North American sporting landscape. The reality show first aired on Spike TV and was the brainchild of Zuffa and Craig Piligian, the producer of Discovery Channel's wildly successful *Dirty Jobs* and *Orange County Choppers*.

The show was an unexpected home run for the UFC, but it required just a little luck. First, the Fertittas were considering selling the UFC because they had lost a substantial amount of money on the property, and while the business was doing a lot better, there was no indication it would achieve the growth they needed to recoup their investment. The fact they decided to invest more money in order to produce *The Ultimate Fighter* showed their dedication to making the series a success.

Second was a little bit of scheduling luck that is rarely mentioned now. The time slot Spike TV chose for the show was right after World Wrestling Entertainment's *RAW* — one of cable television's most highly rated shows. This allowed the UFC to take advantage of a massive lead-in audience of young male viewers. Strangely enough, there were no documented protests from the WWE when this decision was made. Years later, however, it appears that millions of the young male viewers who tuned into *RAW* have switched their allegiances from fake to real fighting. The last bit of luck for the TV show involved the live finale between light heavyweights Forrest Griffin and Stephan Bonnar. The bout turned out to be one of the most exciting fights in UFC history and had 2.6 million people watching, which was, at the time, the largest ever audience for a fight on cable TV.

Since that night in 2005, the UFC has continued to grow at warp speed. It has successfully expanded into Canada, the United Kingdom, Brazil and Germany and is on the verge of running events in places like South Korea, Australia, China, France and Italy. When not growing the business organically, Zuffa has done it through the acquisition of successful promotions like Pride FC, WEC and Strikeforce. And as the Internet has grown, so has the UFC's presence, with the promotion being one of the best at harnessing the power of social media. President Dana White has over 2.8 million Twitter followers, and he instructs all his fighters to set up their own Twitter accounts and "Twitter [their] asses off."

And without much prodding, the fighters themselves have continued to evolve over the 14-plus years that Zuffa has operated the UFC. With better, stronger and smarter athletes, the UFC is always bursting with possibility and has long forgotten the days of 30-minute matches where one man would lie on top of another trying to force a submission. Many of the current crop of fighters were fans of the UFC growing up and have trained specifically as mixed martial artists for years, making them better and more entertaining fighters. And none of this would be important if the fans hadn't also evolved. With MMA gyms becoming commonplace in North America and fights being broadcast regularly on TV, fans are now fight savvy, and their knowledge demands more of fighters, who, in turn, respond by becoming better.

The momentum that began with *The Ultimate Fighter* in 2005 has simply not let up. In early 2010 a company called Flash Entertainment based in Abu Dhabi purchased 10 percent of the UFC for an estimated price north of $100 million. In August 2011 the UFC and Fox announced what may prove to be the most significant deal in UFC history — a seven-year agreement for Fox to air UFC content on its network as well as its FX and Fuel channels. The agreement to air the UFC on Fox marks the first time the promotion has been on a national U.S. network and could be the opportunity the UFC needs to position itself at the same level as iconic sports organizations like the NFL, NBA and Major League Baseball.

Like a good fighter, the UFC was down but not out. And before all is said and done, this Cinderella story might just finish with the UFC becoming the most popular sport in North America.

Enjoy the ride.

Left: Forrest Griffin slugs Stephan Bonnar during *The Ultimate Fighter* season 1 finale on April 9, 2005. Below: Dana White speaks with the media prior to UFC 166 on October 16, 2013.

Chuck Liddell enters the arena to face Wanderlei Silva at UFC 79 in 2007. Liddell defeated Silva via unanimous decision.

LEGENDS

Above and right: Royce Gracie faces off against Matt Hughes at UFC 60 in 2006. Gracie, the UFC's first ever champion, lost to Hughes in what was his second-last professional bout.

HE WASN'T THE biggest, or the best, but he is the most important fighter in the history of mixed martial arts. Royce Gracie was the guy who started it all.

The son of the legendary Helio Gracie, Royce was born into fighting royalty. One of nine kids fathered by Helio — including four boys who became fighters — he was taught Brazilian jiu-jitsu at an early age and was competing in tournaments by the time he turned eight. After earning his blue belt at 17, he joined his brother Rorion in California, helping teach the martial art to Americans.

When Rorion conceived and organized UFC 1, he chose Royce to represent Brazilian jiu-jitsu in the tournament, despite the fact Royce was not considered the toughest of the Gracies. "The others were either too heavy or too light. I just happened to be the right size," explained the 180-pound Royce.

Outweighed by every competitor in the tournament, he used his submission skills to win UFC 1. He also won UFC 2 and 4 and could have won UFC 3 had he not been forced to withdraw because of fatigue after an exhausting first-round match against the hulking Kimo Leopoldo.

Gracie's success centered around his expertise as a ground fighter. Most of his opponents were superior punchers or proficient kickers, but Gracie's jiu-jitsu allowed him to dominate on the mat. Some say his ground skill (or rather, his opponents' lack thereof) was unfair. But ultimately, the most complete fighter was left standing — and Gracie, in the long run, made his contemporaries better by introducing a very effective fighting style. "I wasn't surprised I won because I trained to win," he said. "It may sound cocky but it never surprised me when I won."

For a while, Gracie was unbeatable, going 11-0-1 over a two-year period, all by submission. But the world would catch up. At UFC 5, Gracie and Ken Shamrock fought to a draw. Had the bout been judged, however, Shamrock would have been the clear winner. "I beat the crap out of him," said Shamrock afterward. Gracie took a hiatus following the fight, stating he was unhappy with a number of UFC rule changes that ultimately gave the advantage to strikers.

He didn't return to mixed martial arts until 2000, when he fought Japanese professional wrestler Nobuhiko Takada in the Pride Grand Prix. A pro wrestler, Takada looked tough but wasn't much of a fighter. Gracie easily defeated him but lost in the next round to another Japanese pro wrestler, Kazushi Sakuraba, who unlike Takada, possessed a significant set of skills. It wouldn't be the last time they met.

In 2006, 11 years after he left the UFC, Gracie made his return to the organization. Fighting welterweight Matt Hughes at UFC 60, the bout illustrated just how much the sport had evolved in the previous decade. During his first go-round with the UFC, Gracie toyed with men twice his size. In Hughes, he was facing a lighter opponent, yet despite his size advantage he was outclassed by the American. The fight lasted less than five minutes, with Hughes dominating Gracie in all facets of the match: wrestling, striking and, to add insult to injury, submissions. Hughes locked Gracie in a kimura before finishing him off with multiple unanswered

blows to force a referee stoppage. Gracie may have been overwhelmed that night in the octagon, but he could take comfort in the fact that UFC 60 generated 620,000 pay-per-view buys and became the first event to eclipse the $20 million gross revenue mark.

The final match of Gracie's career was a revenge win over Sakuraba in 2007 in Los Angeles. It would have been a nice bowtie to end his career — however, he tested positive for anabolic steroids after the fight. Gracie disputed the charge but the optics were suspicious: the almost 40-year-old Brazilian had packed on 13 pounds of muscle since the Hughes bout and was boasting a dramatically different-looking physique.

Despite Gracie's mediocre final years, he still carries with him the legacy of being the first true global MMA superstar. Today, all professional mixed martial artists should extend a thank-you to Gracie. The first face of the sport, he set the standard for every fighter who has followed. In 2003 at UFC 45, the UFC honored Gracie by inducting him alongside Ken Shamrock as the first two members of the UFC Hall of Fame.

TALE OF
THE TAPE

BORN

BRAZIL

D.O.B.
1966/12/12

HEIGHT
6'0"

WEIGHT
180 lb.

ASSOCIATION
Gracie
Humaita

NICKNAME
N/A

KEN SHAMROCK

Above: Ken Shamrock prior to his fight at UFC 48 with Kimo Leopoldo. Right: Shamrock lands a punch on Tito Ortiz during their bout at UFC 40 in 2002 – one of the promotion's most important events.

KEN SHAMROCK BEGAN as the UFC's first American superstar and parlayed his reputation and charisma into a pro wrestling and mixed martial arts career that continued all the way into his late forties, establishing himself as one of the biggest names the sport has ever seen.

When Shamrock arrived in Denver for UFC 1, he had no doubt in his mind that he would win the tournament. But he ran into another pretty good submission guy in Royce Gracie, made a mistake, and was choked out. That first career loss wouldn't get Shamrock

down, though. Born Kenneth Wayne Kilpatrick, the young fighter spent his early years in and out of trouble in one of Atlanta's rougher neighborhoods. By the time he was 10 years old his parents had abandoned him. It was an upbringing, he says, that created the inner aggression he took with him into his career.

Salvation came at 14 when he was placed in Bob Shamrock's Boys' Home. It was here he was able to find the structure he needed. By the time he reached high school, he was a star in both football and wrestling and had taken the surname Shamrock to honor his foster father.

Despite an invitation to the San Diego Chargers' NFL training camp, Shamrock chose pro wrestling. That decision landed him in Japan, where he met professional wrestlers Masakatsu Funaki and Minoru Suzuki — the founders of the Pancrase Hybrid Wrestling organization, one of the world's first true fighting promotions. Working with Funaki, Suzuki and catch wrestling guru Karl Gotch, Shamrock quickly picked up the art of submission fighting. By the time he faced Gracie at UFC 1, his record stood at 4-0.

Between 1993 and 1996 his reputation grew as he fought in both UFC and Pancrase. He lost just five of his first 30 bouts, defeating men like Bas Rutten, Kimo Leopoldo and Maurice Smith. But while Shamrock was thriving, the UFC struggled. Political turmoil stirred up by Senator John McCain had devastated the business. Shamrock saw the writing on the wall and followed the money, signing a three-year deal with the World Wrestling Federation in 1997.

Although Shamrock never achieved championship-level stardom with the WWF, he used the exposure to build his own personal brand, playing off his reputation as a successful mixed martial artist by using the nickname "the World's Most Dangerous Man."

He returned to mixed martial arts in 2000, four years older and ready to take on a whole new generation of talented athletes. "It was old school against new school," said Shamrock. "In sport you don't get to see that too often." He may have lost two of four fights upon returning to MMA, but Shamrock still retained an aura of toughness that allowed him to become a major part of one of the most successful and significant pay-per-view events in UFC history.

UFC 40 was headlined by Shamrock and Tito Ortiz. The two had fueled a long-simmering feud that began several years prior at UFC 19, when the pair butted heads over Ortiz's postfight taunting following his win versus Shamrock's friend Guy Mezger. Nothing came of it that night except for some broken furniture, but the incident created a rivalry that helped build tension and drama for UFC 40 in late 2002.

The fight itself was a one-sided affair as the younger, stronger, more technically sound Ortiz won easily, but that really wasn't the story. Since taking over the UFC in 2001, Frank and Lorenzo Fertitta had spent millions of dollars for little return. UFC 40, however, changed the company's fortunes. The sold-out MGM Grand was rockin' that night, and the event secured 150,000 pay-per-view buys, three times larger than the six previous events Zuffa had run since taking over the promotion. It was history repeating itself for Shamrock. The man who had been there at UFC 1, the event that established the Ultimate Fighting Championship, was an integral face at UFC 40, the event that marked the beginning of a new, prosperous era. "Tito Ortiz and myself took MMA and pushed it up to where it is today," said Shamrock. "There's no one who can deny that today."

As a fighter, Ken Shamrock was one of the best when the UFC began. And although his skills declined following UFC 40, he still held mass appeal at the box office and continued to headline major UFC cards, including two more high-profile fights versus Tito Ortiz that helped usher the sport into the modern-day mainstream consciousness. If anyone can say his position as one of the most important figures in the history of mixed martial arts is secure, it's Shamrock.

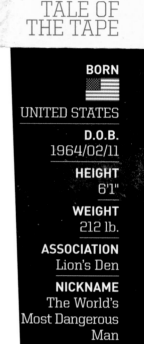

TALE OF THE TAPE

BORN

UNITED STATES

D.O.B.
1964/02/11

HEIGHT
6'1"

WEIGHT
212 lb.

ASSOCIATION
Lion's Den

NICKNAME
The World's Most Dangerous Man

KAZUSHI SAKURABA

Above: Kazushi Sakuraba works to submit Kestutis Smirnovas in his win at K1 Hero's 6 in 2006.
Right: Sakuraba stomps on Antonio Schembri during their bout at Pride 25 in 2003.

OF ALL THE Japanese fighters who have taken part in MMA over the past 25 years, it is Kazushi Sakuraba who gets the most credit for the popularity of the sport in his native country. "He was a huge superstar," UFC president Dana White said. "He definitely put mixed martial arts on the map in Japan and the rest of the world." For fans, he'll be remembered as a larger-than-life character who took on anybody and everybody during a storied career, changing the course of MMA in the process.

As with many Japanese fighters, Sakuraba was a product of professional wrestling. He came up through the Union of Wrestling Forces International organization, where Billy Robinson trained him in the art of catch wrestling. His wrestling career was respectable but undistinguished, and Sakuraba made a name for himself only when he began fighting for real.

His first MMA bout came against Kimo Leopoldo. The fight featured two of the characteristics that would become synonymous with a Sakuraba match: a significant size advantage and controversy. The larger Leopoldo won, but there was evidence to suggest the fight was a "work," or the final outcome had been scripted. In hindsight, Sakuraba could have pressed an advantage many times and possibly submitted the Hawaiian. Leopoldo always insisted he won fairly, but Sakuraba has never commented on the fight and later became far and away the more skilled fighter.

Sakuraba's second bout took place in 1997, and again his 6 feet and 177 pounds were badly mismatched — this time against the 6-foot-3, 240-pound giant Marcus "Conan" Silveira. Controversy reared its ugly head when referee "Big" John McCarthy prematurely stopped the match, with Sakuraba losing (it was later ruled no contest). The pair fought again the same night, and Sakuraba won by submission. Over the next two years the former pro wrestler proved that his triumph over Silveira was no fluke when he posted wins over former UFC champions Carlos Newton, Guy Mezger and Vitor Belfort.

Impressive victories aside, it was Sakuraba's showing during the final round of the mammoth Pride Grand Prix 2000 that cemented his legendary status among Japanese fans. In his first bout of the eight-man tournament, promoters ensured Sakuraba would face the legendary Royce Gracie, who was fighting for the first time since leaving the UFC five years earlier. Given the long layoff, Gracie and his handlers were cautious to the point of absurdity when it came to deciding who Royce would fight. In Sakuraba, they felt they had a name opponent whom Gracie could handle while earning a sizable payday. However, once the bout started it was clear Sakuraba was stronger and more technically sound than Gracie. Over the course of six 15-minute rounds, the Japanese fighter bested the Brazilian both standing up and on the ground. Royce's brother Rorion threw in the towel. Sakuraba had defeated the mighty Brazilian and would forever be known as "the Gracie Hunter."

His quarterfinal win over Gracie vaulted him to a semifinal match against Igor Vovchanchyn, at the time the hardest-hitting heavyweight in the world. The Ukrainian had nearly 50 pounds on Sakuraba, who was exhausted from the Gracie fight. The Japanese star rose to the challenge, but despite equaling the Ukrainian for two rounds, he conceded the fight because of fatigue.

Over the ensuing years, Sakuraba's legend grew in Pride, but it came at a price. Unlike in North America, where winning is the most admired quality of a fighter, Japanese fight fans value courage and a willingness to fight any opponent above all. The Japanese promoters had no trouble playing to this bias and continually matched Sakuraba with the biggest and the best. Amazingly, the 177-pounder defeated UFC champions like Quinton Jackson and Kevin Randleman, both highly skilled fighters who outweighed him by 30 to 40 pounds, by utilizing an array of submission skills and his wrestling acumen. He also lost to championship-caliber fighters such as Wanderlei Silva (twice), Mirko Filipovic, Antonio Rogerio Nogueira and Melvin Manhoef, nearly all of them savage strikers who dished out serious beatings that likely shortened Sakuraba's career. By 2007, with his skills fading, he lost a rematch against Royce Gracie. However the results of that bout were overturned when Gracie tested positive for a banned substance.

Sakuraba lost his last four fights, and as of early 2014 had not stepped into the ring in three years. He hasn't announced his official retirement, but it's safe to say, barring a miraculous comeback, his competitive fighting career is over. He leaves an amazing legacy and will be forever remembered as Japan's number one star in mixed martial arts.

TALE OF
THE TAPE

BORN

JAPAN

D.O.B.
1969/07/14

HEIGHT
6'0"

WEIGHT
177 lb.

ASSOCIATION
Laughter7

NICKNAME
The Gracie
Hunter

MASAKATSU FUNAKI

Above: Masakatsu Funaki submits Ikuhisa Minowa by heel hook at Dream 6 in Saitama, Japan, in 2008. Right: Funaki punches Rickson Gracie at C2K Colosseum 2000 on May 26, 2000.

KAZUSHI SAKURABA MAY be the biggest name when it comes to Japanese mixed martial arts legends, but Masakatsu Funaki is the man who put the sport on the map in Japan and the first Japanese MMA superstar in the modern era.

Like many early Japanese mixed martial artists, Funaki, with his rock star looks and exuberance in the ring, came from the world of pro wrestling. In his case, New Japan Pro-Wrestling, an organization known for realistic-looking matches. All New Japan wrestlers were taught the art of catch (or

submission) wrestling as part of their training, which is where Funaki began his journey to stardom as a teenager.

In 1993, he and fellow wrestler Minoru Suzuki created Pancrase, one of Japan's first mixed martial arts promotions. With Funaki as its poster boy, the organization grew quickly. He faced one of his protégés, American Ken Shamrock, in Pancrase's first title match in September 1993, and although the Japanese fighter lost, he would go on to win 12 of his next 13 bouts, submitting such luminaries as Bas Rutten by toe hold, Vernon

White by palm strike and Shamrock in their rematch by rear naked choke. "It was very, very difficult to train for him," said Shamrock. "Obviously, he kind of taught me everything I knew so it was tough to get in there and fight him because there was nothing I was going to show him that was new."

Business with Pancrase was strong for several years, but success took its toll. Besides running the promotion, Funaki, the organization's number one star, also appeared on most cards. During Pancrase's first year he fought 11 times — a grueling schedule considering present-day elite fighters compete just two or three times a year. And Funaki was more than willing to take a beating to win a bout.

As promoter of the events, Funaki also had to ensure that his matches were entertaining, a mandate made especially difficult when he faced a fighter of lesser ability. Funaki and Suzuki often took it easy on their opponents so that bouts would appear more competitive and entertaining. According to former UFC and Pancrase champion Frank Shamrock, "[Funaki and Suzuki] were light years ahead of everyone else, and they were so good they would go towards entertainment before finishing off a match."

Funaki announced his retirement in 1999 but was back one year later to face Brazilian legend Rickson Gracie. Rickson was known for being MMA legend Royce Gracie's older brother and, allegedly, having a 400-0 record as a street fighter — a dubious claim at best. Still there was no doubt that Rickson was a tough guy and a world-class grappler.

The match was eagerly anticipated by the Japanese public. Funaki walked into the Tokyo Dome dressed as a samurai, replete with sword at his side, and an estimated 30 million watched on television as Rickson blew out Funaki's knee with a kick, then submitted him with a choke hold. Funaki, his pride on the line in front of a hometown crowd, refused to tap and actually passed out before the referee stopped the fight.

Following the bout, Funaki retired once again and was honored at a Pancrase event

later that year. This time he stayed on the sidelines for seven years until he once again agreed to come out of retirement for another "dream matchup."

His opponent? Kazushi Sakuraba. Together, Sakuraba and Funaki are considered the two greatest Japanese mixed martial artists of all time. Prior to the match Funaki claimed that, despite his age, he was ready for the fight. "My recovery is a bit slower than before and you must think I'm lying but I am now stronger than before." Both men were clearly past their prime, but the matchup didn't disappoint the fans who had packed the Kyocera Dome on New Year's Eve 2007. Funaki appeared fit and his punches quicker and crisper than those of Sakuraba. However, the younger man took Funaki to the ground and eventually submitted him with a wrist lock.

Funaki fought three more times and then retired for a third, and seemingly final, time in 2012 with a record of 39-13-2. He left a huge mark on the sport — as a pioneer, a gifted fighter and a charismatic star who played a significant and undeniable role in the growth of mixed martial arts in Japan.

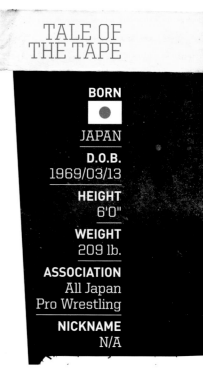

TALE OF THE TAPE

BORN
JAPAN

D.O.B.
1969/03/13

HEIGHT
6'0"

WEIGHT
209 lb.

ASSOCIATION
All Japan
Pro Wrestling

NICKNAME
N/A

BAS RUTTEN

Above and right: Bas Rutten squares off against Tsuyoshi Kosaka at UFC 18: Road to the Heavyweight Title, in 1999. Rutten defeated Kosaka and then defeated Kevin Randleman for the heavyweight title at UFC 20.

TODAY BAS RUTTEN is known by many as the wacky MMA television commentator with a European accent willing to do anything for a laugh. But the reality is "El Guapo" remains one of the most underrated all-time greats. A hardened fighter who cut his teeth in an elite but obscure circuit, had he fought more often in North America he'd probably be remembered with luminaries like Ken Shamrock. As it is, Rutten is still one of the best to ever put on a pair of grappling gloves.

Born to a middle-class family in Holland, Rutten suffered from both eczema and asthma as a child. His poor health and frail body made walks to and from school an exercise in survival, and he was often bullied.

Fortunately, life changed for Rutten at the age of 12 while on holiday in France. Although underage, he and his older brother managed to sneak into a movie theater to watch the classic Bruce Lee movie *Enter the Dragon*. The movie enthralled the young Dutchman, who began begging his conservative parents to allow him to study martial arts. When they finally relented, the naturally gifted fighter immersed himself in the study of taekwondo and was soon able to settle an old score with one of his childhood bullies.

He later launched a professional kickboxing career, quickly building a 14-2 record. "His kickboxing was devastating. It was something everybody feared," remembered Frank Shamrock, who lost two of three fights against Rutten. His skill attracted international attention, and he was invited to join the Pancrase organization in Japan. It was a risky decision — Pancrase allowed grappling and kicking but only open-hand punching. For an accomplished striker like Rutten, the inability to strike an opponent closed-handed should have been a disadvantage, especially when facing seasoned ground fighters. Rutten, however, was so good with his hands that he still managed to defeat many premier Pancrase fighters, including household name Masakatsu Funaki, breaking the Japanese wrestler's cheekbone and nose during their lengthy war.

In 1998 Rutten decided to try his luck in the UFC. After a title fight with heavyweight champion Randy Couture fell through, Rutten beat Tsuyoshi Kosaka at UFC 18 to set up a heavyweight title fight with Kevin Randleman. Although Rutten spent much of the bout on his back trying to defend himself from Randleman's ground and pound attack, judges believed he landed enough punches to earn a very controversial split decision. Twelve months later, years of training and fighting caught up with him, and Rutten was advised by doctors to retire, having suffered serious injuries to his knee, biceps and neck.

In retirement, Rutten used his natural charisma and familiarity with the Japanese fight scene to secure a job as the color commentator for the English broadcasts of the Pride Fighting Championships. Although he lacked the polish of most on-air personalities, Rutten made up for it with credibility, enthusiasm and a quirky sense of humor. While analyzing a fighter he once commented, "Hopefully he plays his card right — or should I say cards — hopefully

he has more than one!" Later he and Kenny Rice hosted a weekly show for the short-lived International Fight League, and since 2009 he and Rice have fronted the long-running *Inside MMA* show. He also released an assortment of training, self-defense and workout videos.

As a fighter, Rutten amassed a 28-4-1 record, including wins over big-name fighters like Frank Shamrock, Guy Mezger and Funaki, ending his career on a 22-fight win streak.

It's a remarkable stat that many don't consider when discussing all-time greats. Even the renowned striker's versatility is often forgotten. "If you look at my record you'll see I actually won more fights by submission than KO," Rutten said. "Also every submission or KO came in different ways — KO to liver, head, palm strikes, etc. Also, submissions — heel hooks, toe holds, kimura, straight arm-bars etc." Unfortunately, Rutten's best fighting was done in Japan, and when he did make it to the UFC at the turn of the millennium, the organization had a very small fan base.

Despite the bad timing, no one should feel sorry for Rutten. He carved out a tremendous postretirement career. Those who take the time to watch some of his old battles will quickly realize he belongs in an elite group with MMA's legendary pioneers.

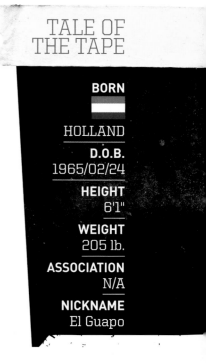

TALE OF THE TAPE

BORN

HOLLAND

D.O.B.
1965/02/24

HEIGHT
6'1"

WEIGHT
205 lb.

ASSOCIATION
N/A

NICKNAME
El Guapo

TANK ABBOTT

Above: Tank Abbott punches Wesley Correira during their bout at UFC 45 in 2003. Abbott lost, but avenged his defeat two years later at Rumble on the Rock 7. Right: Abbott punches Frank Mir at UFC 41 on February 28, 2003 – his first bout since 1998.

ON THE SURFACE, it's difficult to call a one-dimensional fighter with a 10-16 lifetime record a legend, but set aside wins and skill in favor of historical importance and the ability to entertain, and David "Tank" Abbott surely must be given a place on that list.

Tank Abbott's importance was as much about the character he developed as it was about his ability as a fighter. In the early days of the UFC, part of the allure was watching fighters from different disciplines pitted against each other to judge who was using the most effective of the martial arts. Royce Gra-

cie represented Brazilian jiu-jitsu; Dan Severn represented wrestling; Tank Abbott, who claimed to be a veteran of several hundred bar fights, represented the average Joe. He called himself a pit fighter, implying he had no special training other than a habit of finding trouble in all the wrong places.

To understand Abbott, his very first mixed martial arts bout is a good start. It was July 14, 1995, UFC 6, and his opponent was John Matua, an expert in Kapu Kuialua, the Hawaiian martial art based on bone breaking, joint locks and throws.

Tank wasted no time with Matua and began swinging with abandon as soon as the fight started. Matua managed to get his face in front of the majority of Tank's haymakers, and after 20 seconds referee "Big" John McCarthy pulled Tank off the near-unconscious Matua to end the fight. The beatdown and Tank's postfight comments went a long way to establishing his heel persona. "I'm starting to get sexually aroused right now," he told a shocked pay-per-view audience as he reviewed a replay of the fight. "So you better turn that off now."

Away from the octagon, Tank did little to detract from his reputation. With his prominent goatee and belly, he loved being the heel, making him an instant fan favorite with the American audience.

Even when he wasn't competing, Tank could be found stirring the pot, as he did at UFC 8 in Puerto Rico. That night he initiated a postevent scrap with Brazilian middleweight Allan Goes, and after the two were separated, he used some choice words to insult Elaine McCarthy, the wife of referee Big John. That led to the McCarthys giving the UFC an "it's us or him" ultimatum. The UFC chose Big John, and Tank earned some paid time off.

Because of his larger-than-life personality, many forget that Tank was actually pretty decent at his chosen craft. During his prime years, good technical fighters were at a premium, so Tank's formidable knockout power, willingness to give and receive punishment and underrated athleticism — he was a decent amateur wrestler — made him a dangerous opponent.

In addition, his popularity was enhanced by the way he scrapped. His wins and losses always seemed to be dramatic. Twice he lost in the finals of eight-man tournaments (in UFC 6 versus Oleg Taktarov and in Ultimate Ultimate 1996 versus Don Frye), and both times he held the early advantage only to see victory slip away because of his poor cardio. It was the same story when he lost to UFC heavyweight champion Maurice Smith at UFC 15; he controlled the early action but eventually ran out of gas.

His bad boy reputation and marketability actually kept his career going longer than it probably should have. In fact, he ended up winning just two of his last 11 professional fights — an indicator that his reputation lasted significantly longer than his true ability. Tank earned a decent payday fighting YouTube sensation Kimbo Slice, but it didn't impress one viewer. "I thought the whole thing was a farce," said UFC president Dana White. "I love Tank, but I don't want to see that again."

In 2011, Abbott fought Scott Ferrozzo, a man he originally met in 1996. Seventeen years after their first encounter, with both men sporting a few extra pounds and multiple gray hairs, the two engaged in a "backyard brawl." Tank won the unsanctioned rematch, spurring him to enter a King of the Cage bout in 2013 versus Ruben Villareal, who took no mercy on the aging veteran and pummeled Abbott in the second round. Hopefully, for the sake of Abbott's legacy, it will end up being the final chapter of one of mixed martial arts' most notorious careers.

TALE OF THE TAPE

BORN
UNITED STATES
D.O.B.
1965/04/26
HEIGHT
6'0"
WEIGHT
250 lb.
ASSOCIATION
N/A
NICKNAME
Tank

RANDY COUTURE

Above: Randy Couture punches Brandon Vera in his unanimous victory at UFC 105 in 2009. Right: Couture submits Mark Coleman at UFC 109 in 2010.

RANDY COUTURE PUT his name on the mixed martial arts map by excelling when it mattered most. His ability to win big fights along with his all-American good-guy charisma created a legacy that few can match.

Before becoming a fighter, Couture spent six years in the U.S. Army, rising to the level of sergeant in the 101st U.S. Airborne Division. He then attended Oklahoma State University, where he was a three-time All-American and two-time runner-up in the NCAA's 190-pound division. He also won gold at the Pan Am Games and was a

three-time alternate for the American Olympic Team.

Couture established an early reputation as a fighter capable of rising to the occasion. At UFC 15 in 1997, just his third professional bout, he faced off against Brazilian superstar Vitor Belfort. Belfort was the overwhelming favorite, having just ripped through the UFC heavyweight division using a rapid-fire, two-fisted attack to dispatch fighters much larger than himself. But using guile and a strategy surprising for someone who had just two professional fights under his belt, Couture subdued Belfort with superior wrestling skills, eventually winning by TKO at 8:17 of the fight. The victory that night in Mississippi was a huge upset and endeared Couture to American fans, who loved that the Army veteran had used a mix of brains and brawn to defeat the dangerous Brazilian striker.

The win catapulted the Washington native to a title shot against heavyweight champion Maurice Smith. The two met at UFC Japan, and Couture again dominated using his vastly superior wrestling, winning the first of his five UFC titles.

Having been in all of four professional North American fights, Couture vacated the UFC title to try his hand in the Japanese pro loop, going 2-2. The UFC invited him back in 2000 for a heavyweight title shot against champion Kevin Randleman. It was another opportunity for Couture to rise to the occasion. In Randleman, Couture was facing a fellow wrestler with skills equal to his own. For the first two rounds, Randleman used those skills to control the fight. But Couture had evolved in Japan and stayed alive by employing an excellent guard against his seasoned adversary. When his opponent began to tire Couture took advantage, putting Randleman on his back and raining down with ground and pound offense. Referee John McCarthy stopped the bout at 4:13 of the third round, and Randy Couture was UFC heavyweight champion once again.

Couture defended his title twice against Brazilian Pedro Rizzo before meeting Josh Barnett in UFC 36 as the betting favorite. Barnett weighed in at 243 pounds; Couture was 226. The 17-pound advantage combined with Barnett's significant striking and grappling abilities was too much for Couture, and the star lost his belt. After another defeat against a significantly larger opponent, Ricco Rodriguez, Couture dropped his fighting weight to 205 pounds and joined the light heavyweight division.

With the move came the opportunity to square off against Chuck Liddell for the vacant UFC light heavyweight title. Couture held off the hard-hitting Liddell for several rounds, took him to the ground in the third and pounded out a TKO to earn the belt. With the victory, Couture became the first fighter ever to win UFC titles in two divisions.

Belfort and Liddell would end up as Couture's biggest rivals — and both would score redemption wins against the champ. Couture settled the score against Belfort, winning the third fight of their trilogy, but Liddell was a different story. The fellow American bested Couture, and after the loss to Liddell, the former Army sergeant announced his retirement to a supportive crowd at the Mandalay Bay in Las Vegas in 2006. At 42 years old, he had simply fought enough — or so he had thought.

Inexplicably, 13 months later, Couture was back in the octagon and up a weight class, challenging Tim Sylvia for the UFC heavyweight title. Despite giving up seven inches in height, 50 pounds in weight and 13 years in age, Couture stunned the champion with a straight right hand seven seconds into the bout for his third heavyweight title.

Couture continued fighting for four more years, defending his title once and going 4-3 until a nasty front kick from light heavyweight Lyoto Machida knocked him out for good. It was enough to convince the 47-year-old he'd finally had enough — but with roles in action movies such as *The Expendables* in his post-MMA career, it won't be the last we'll see of the legendary fighter, proving his charisma extends far beyond the octagon.

TALE OF THE TAPE

BORN

UNITED STATES

D.O.B.
1963/06/22

HEIGHT
6'1"

WEIGHT
205 lb.

ASSOCIATION
Xtreme Couture

NICKNAME
The Natural

MARK COLEMAN

Above and right: Mark Coleman defeats Stephan Bonnar by unanimous decision at UFC 100 on July 11, 2009. The bout was the last victory of Coleman's career.

THE FIRST UFC heavyweight champion and the pioneer of ground and pound, Mark Coleman, the wrestler from Ohio nicknamed "the Hammer," changed mixed martial arts forever.

Coleman made a stunning entrance into the UFC after a spectacular amateur wrestling career that saw him win an NCAA championship, finish second at the 1991 freestyle world championships and earn a spot on the 1992 U.S. Olympic Team. He won tournaments in both UFC 10 and UFC 11. His success was achieved through a ground and pound style, where he used his prodigious wrestling skills to take down and mount his opponent. Once on top, he'd rain down punches, head butts (made illegal after UFC 14, no thanks to Coleman himself) and shoulder strikes while controlling the match with superior positioning and strength.

Coleman's aggression and amazing strength overwhelmed strikers and submission experts. Prior to his arrival it was widely accepted that Royce Gracie's Brazilian jiu-jitsu was the most effective martial art. That theory changed after Coleman's six straight UFC wins, including three fights in one night at UFC 10 and his win versus Dan Severn at UFC 12 to become the organization's first heavyweight champion. He seemed unstoppable, and many people believed defeating an aggressive world-class wrestler like Coleman was virtually impossible. Until Maurice Smith came along.

It was anticipated that Coleman would dominate Maurice Smith at UFC 14. Smith, one of the best kickboxers in the world at the time, wasn't expected to be able to deal with Coleman's powerful wrestling skills. Smith, however, began training in preparation for Coleman with Frank Shamrock. The veteran fighter improved Smith's conditioning and grappling defense — in particular, a position called "the guard." Although jiu-jitsu fighters use the guard as a starting point for various submission holds, it is also a very effective defensive maneuver. It's employed when the man on the bottom wraps his legs around his opponent's trunk. At the same time he uses his arms to keep his opponent close, making it impossible for the fighter on top to get enough distance to throw effective strikes.

Once the fight started, Coleman, as expected, easily took Smith down and began employing his ground and pound attack. However, Smith, using his guard to perfection, suffered very little damage. By the time 15 minutes of regular time had expired, Coleman was exhausted while Smith was relatively fresh, having thrown and absorbed very few punches. Smith's game plan was a horizontal version of Muhammad Ali's infamous rope-a-dope gamesmanship, and in overtime Smith simply overwhelmed Coleman. The kickboxer earned a unanimous decision and the UFC heavyweight championship. "I thought I was going to take this guy down and pound his ass out," said Coleman. "But he had a hell of a coach in Frank Shamrock and a hell of a game plan."

A generation of up-and-coming fighters took notice — there was no longer one dominant martial art. Instead, more often than not, victory would go to the well-rounded fighter who could adapt to any situation.

The loss to Smith was the first of four in a row for Coleman, including a controversial decision to Pedro Rizzo at UFC 18 and a shocking submission loss to Japanese pro wrestler Nobuhiko Takada at Pride 5. When rumors arose that Coleman had thrown the fight, his only response was to say he "needed to support his family."

It appeared Coleman was entering the final stage of a career highlighted by victories at UFC 10, 11 and 12 and his reputation as the master of the ground and pound. But on May 1, 2000, he shocked the MMA community, defeating three opponents in one night, including Igor Vovchanchyn, the number one fighter in the world at that time, to capture the Pride Grand Prix 2000. It was the biggest win of Coleman's MMA career. "If you saw my celebration afterwards — it was euphoria — I couldn't see straight," he recalled years later. "I just jumped right out of the ring."

Emboldened by his win, Coleman fought until 2009 before retiring after a loss to perennial UFC champion Randy Couture. His final win, at UFC 100 over Stephan Bonnar, was 13 years less a day from his first fight in the UFC. It was a fitting performance at one of the UFC's prestigious events by a man who will go down as one of the best, and most historically significant, fighters in MMA history.

TALE OF
THE TAPE

BORN

UNITED STATES

D.O.B.
1964/12/20

HEIGHT
6'1"

WEIGHT
205 lb.

ASSOCIATION
Hammer
House

NICKNAME
The Hammer

MATT HUGHES

Above: Matt Hughes defends his welterweight title against BJ Penn at UFC 63 in 2006. Right: Hughes defeats Matt Serra in the Fight of the Night at UFC 98 in 2009.

MATT HUGHES OFTEN entered his fights accompanied by the strains of the song "A Country Boy Will Survive." It's an appropriate tune for a fighter who not only survived an extraordinary length of time as a dominant UFC welterweight but also thrived, defeating many dangerous opponents in dramatic style.

Born and raised on a farm in Hillsboro, Illinois, Hughes was the prototypical "country strong" combatant. His early years were spent working on the family farm for a demanding father. "He was very motivating," recalled Matt. "He and his belt, that is." The work ethic

he learned on the farm helped him become a high school wrestling star and, later, an All-America wrestler at Eastern Illinois University.

He took up mixed martial arts after university, fighting the majority of his bouts in Extreme Challenge. His early success was built on his wrestling skills and amazing physical strength, qualities that helped him post a remarkable 29-3 record prior to challenging for the UFC welterweight championship at UFC 34.

In one of the most exciting fights in UFC history, Hughes took on Canadian jiu-jitsu master Carlos Newton. Early in the second round, Newton caught Hughes with a triangle choke from his back. In an effort to break the choke, Hughes picked up Newton and carried him to the octagon wall with Newton's legs still wrapped around his neck. Newton, now pressed against the side of the cage, continued to apply the choke. As Hughes was losing consciousness he used his final ounce of strength to slam the Canadian to the ground. The force of the slam not only broke the hold but knocked Newton out cold. Hughes, who later admitted he too nearly lost consciousness, was declared the winner.

In his next match he defeated the favored Hayato Sakurai via unanimous decision at UFC 36. At the time Sakurai had an impressive 18-1-2 record, his only loss coming to the man now considered one of the best pound-for-pound fighters of all time, Anderson Silva.

Hughes lost the title at UFC 46 when he was submitted by Hawaiian-born BJ Penn. It would be the first of three contests against "the Prodigy," one of the most talented fighters of all time. Penn later vacated the title because of a legal dispute with the UFC, and the belt ended up around the waist of Georges St-Pierre, whom Hughes defeated to regain the title at UFC 50. Like Penn, St-Pierre became one of Hughes' great rivals, as they too would end up with a memorable trilogy of fights.

UFC 52 went down as one of Hughes' most dramatic victories. Frank Trigg was one of the few opponents Hughes admitted to disliking. "He was a big talker and I'm not a big talker," Hughes said. During their second fight, Hughes was left gasping for breath by a kick to the groin. When he turned to complain to referee Mario Yamasaki, Trigg began throwing punches until finally taking Hughes to the ground and locking him in a rear naked choke hold. For over two minutes Hughes fought off the submission attempt, and then, in one of the most dramatic moments in UFC history, lifted Trigg off the ground and gave him a thunderous slam. Appropriately, Hughes administered his own rear naked choke to end the fight.

Hughes was given a chance to avenge his loss to BJ Penn — his only defeat over a 19-fight stretch — at UFC 63. Penn looked the better fighter in the early going, but he injured his ribs in the second round and Hughes took control in the third, winning by TKO. By avenging his most important loss, Hughes' victory over Penn became arguably the crowning achievement of his career.

But time was one of the few opponents Hughes knew he'd never beat, and after losing his next match to St-Pierre, he lost four of eight and called it a career in 2011. "I kept getting older and the guys I seemed to be facing stayed at 28 or 29," he said about his decision. The free time allowed Hughes to pen a book, *Made in America: The Most Dominant Champion in UFC History*, and reflect on his career.

Hughes retired with a 45-9 record as one of the sport's most consistent and dramatic performers. UFC president Dana White once proclaimed Hughes–Trigg at UFC 52 to be his personal favorite fight. Now that the country boy has ridden off into the sunset, the familiar twang of his entrance song is no longer heard, but his legend only grows stronger.

TALE OF THE TAPE

BORN

UNITED STATES

D.O.B.
1973/10/13

HEIGHT
5'9"

WEIGHT
170 lb.

ASSOCIATION
Hit Squad

NICKNAME
N/A

CHUCK LIDDELL

Above: Chuck Liddell defeats Randy Couture at UFC 52 for the light heavyweight championship. Right: Liddell defends his title against Tito Ortiz at UFC 66 on December 30, 2006.

CHUCK LIDDELL NEEDS no introduction. His face and trademark fauxhawk have been part of the UFC brand for nearly 20 years. A formidable fighter during his era, Liddell helped usher the UFC into the mainstream, becoming the darling of the promotion during his long tenure.

Born in 1969, the California native was an early study of karate, specifically Koei-Kan (a tattoo representing the discipline can be seen on his head). He added football and wrestling to his athletic arsenal and ended up on the Cal Tech Division I wrestling team.

Although it took several tune-up fights for the light heavyweight to find his groove once he joined the UFC, Liddell settled in, running up a 12-1 professional record over a four-year period between 1998 and 2002. Highlights for "the Iceman" included a first-round stoppage versus former champion Kevin Randleman at UFC 31 and a unanimous victory over Vitor Belfort at UFC 37.5. During the bout, Liddell showcased "the wall walk," a technique he popularized to stuff an opponent while in guard. While on the mat in a defensive position, Liddell would simply wriggle against the cage and voilà — back on his feet in no time.

When he met a 39-year-old Randy Couture at UFC 43, all bets were on Liddell. Couture was old and coming off two straight losses. Liddell had won 10 in a row. As the fight began, Liddell fired a low kick at Couture, who summarily rejected the attempt and rushed at the younger fighter, pushing him against the wall and slamming him down. Liddell was spent by the third round and Couture pounced, gaining top position and hammering away. In what should have been a step toward a title shot, Liddell took a step back, but he learned important lessons that would set up one of the most hyped rematches in UFC history three years later.

First, though, Liddell represented the UFC at the 2003 Pride Middleweight Grand Prix in Japan. When he returned to North America to face Tito Ortiz at UFC 47, he was hungrier than ever. The two never liked each other, and after Liddell dusted the popular former champion, Ortiz accused the Iceman of eye gouging. It wasn't the first time the allegation had surfaced among MMA fighters, and Liddell earned a reputation as "the Eyesman" for his less than sportsmanlike maneuver.

Whereas Couture and Liddell's first bout did reasonably well — 49,000 pay-per-view buys, $645,000 at the gate — UFC 57 came on the heels of the first season of *The Ultimate Fighter*. The reality TV show featured both men as opposing coaches, and its ratings and format rocketed MMA into the mainstream. The subsequent match that pitted the two coaches against each other confirmed it, raking in six times the amount of PPV buys and $2,000,000 in ticket sales. And the fight was worth it: Liddell made adjustments in the rematch, increasing his footwork and lateral movement and sharpening his striking. At 2:06 of the first, the ref intervened after Liddell dropped a bomb to win the light heavyweight championship. He defended the belt against Jeremy Horn four months later before facing the aging Couture once again in early 2006 to complete their trilogy. It ended in similar fashion, with Liddell scoring a knockout win.

In many ways, Couture's demise made Liddell who he was and secured the new champion's place at the top of the light heavyweight heap.

The Iceman defended his title twice more, including a decisive KO of Renato Sobral and a rematch with Ortiz that ranks in the UFC's top 5 all-time in PPV buys. But Liddell was about to meet his undoing in Quinton "Rampage" Jackson.

Liddell had already lost once to Jackson when he made his trip to Japan, and their rematch marked the beginning of the end for the Iceman as Rampage KO'd the champ in the first round at UFC 71. Although he'd put up a scrap for the ages versus Wanderlei Silva at UFC 79 in late 2007, earning Fight of the Night honors, it would be Liddell's final moment of victory in the octagon.

The hard-striking Californian amassed the second most KOs in UFC history, and although the warrior bowed out with three losses to finish his MMA career at 21-8, Liddell's legacy remains intact. Since then, his popularity has never abated. Transitioning his mass appeal, Liddell has appeared on *Dancing With the Stars*, regularly works with UFC management as an ambassador and maintains several sponsorship deals. In a sport populated with memorable names, Liddell's ranks high for his knockout power and all-American appeal.

TALE OF THE TAPE

BORN
UNITED STATES

D.O.B.
1969/12/17

HEIGHT
6'2"

WEIGHT
205 lb.

ASSOCIATION
The Pit

NICKNAME
The Iceman

Light heavyweight Daniel Cormier throws Dan Henderson at UFC 173 on May 24, 2014.
Cormier won the bout by submission in the third round.

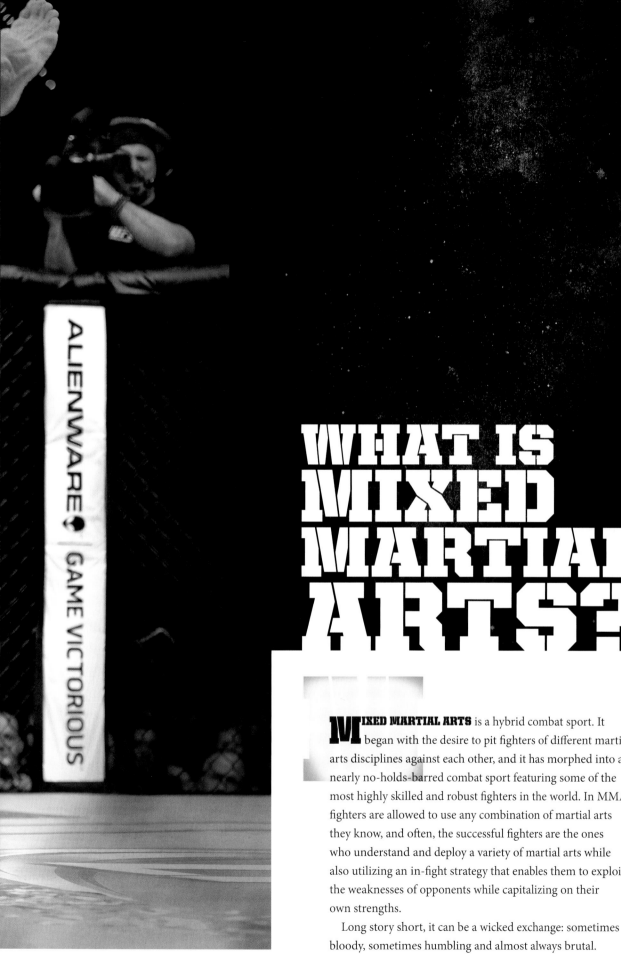

ALIENWARE | GAME VICTORIOUS

WHAT IS MIXED MARTIAL ARTS?

MIXED MARTIAL ARTS is a hybrid combat sport. It began with the desire to pit fighters of different martial arts disciplines against each other, and it has morphed into a nearly no-holds-barred combat sport featuring some of the most highly skilled and robust fighters in the world. In MMA, fighters are allowed to use any combination of martial arts they know, and often, the successful fighters are the ones who understand and deploy a variety of martial arts while also utilizing an in-fight strategy that enables them to exploit the weaknesses of opponents while capitalizing on their own strengths.

Long story short, it can be a wicked exchange: sometimes bloody, sometimes humbling and almost always brutal.

Examples of MMA disciplines (clockwise from left): boxing, jiu-jitsu, wrestling and kickboxing.

POPULAR DISCIPLINES

Although many types of martial arts are used in MMA, the following are the most predominant:

BOXING

Think Muhammad Ali, Mike Tyson, Manny Pacquiao and Floyd Mayweather. For a very long time in American and European history, boxing was the fighting style of choice to establish the might of men. In boxing, participants throw punches at one another. All punches are legal except those that land below the waist or those considered to be rabbit punches — ones that land on the back of the neck and top of the spine and may cause spinal damage.

Many MMA fighters are excellent boxers, such as Anderson Silva, Nick Diaz and Johny Hendricks. All that being said, none of these men are skilled enough to entertain a title fight with an elite-level boxer. On the other hand, there are fighters like Alessio Sakara and K.J. Noons who came to MMA after legitimate boxing careers.

WRESTLING

Wrestling, just like at the Olympics, involves controlling and taking an opponent down to the mat. As such, it can be argued that wrestling is the most important discipline in mixed martial arts. It involves balance, strength, stamina and explosive power that allows fighters to overtake opponents and mount them, either for submission or for ground and pound offense.

An accomplished wrestler can wreak havoc in the ring, and the importance of the discipline in MMA is supported by the fact that wrestling is the background of more UFC champions than any other martial art. Some of MMA's most notable champions who come from the wrestling world are Mark Coleman, Kevin Randleman, Tito Ortiz, Matt Hughes, Randy Couture, Jon Jones, Gray Maynard and Benson Henderson.

KICKBOXING

Kickboxing and its related disciplines like Muay Thai and taekwondo are martial arts that allow both punching and

kicking. As in boxing, it's illegal to kick or punch below the belt, and rabbit punches are also prohibited. Although kickboxing is an extremely useful skill in MMA, most successful fighters who come from this discipline need to have at least a basic proficiency at wrestling, in particular a technique known as "the sprawl." This is when a fighter spreads his legs and uses his balance to avoid being taken to the mat. Perennial light heavyweight champion Chuck Liddell was a competent collegiate wrestler who became an excellent kickboxer. He used his wrestling base to keep many of his fights against superior wrestlers like Randy Couture and Tito Ortiz "standing up" so he could exploit his advantage as a striker.

CATCH WRESTLING
Catch wrestling is a variation of wrestling that features a combination of wrestling techniques and submission holds. It is well known and utilized in Japan but not as common in North America.

Japanese wrestler Antonio Inoki was an early adopter of catch wrestling, as were Ken and Frank Shamrock. Current heavyweight standout Josh Barnett, who often trains in Japan, identifies himself as a catch wrestler.

BRAZILIAN JIU-JITSU
Brazilian jiu-jitsu emphasizes ground fighting and submission holds. It is similar in some ways to catch wrestling; however, it is not nearly as aggressive. BJJ techniques encourage a slow and methodical approach to creating positions that lead to submissions. Royce Gracie introduced the discipline to North American audiences. Since then many Brazilian and non-Brazilian fighters have demonstrated its effectiveness. UFC champions BJ Penn, Frank Mir and Carlos Newton are some of the more accomplished jiu-jitsu artists.

JUDO
Although not usually talked about as much as some of the other disciplines, judo has proved itself surprisingly effective in the MMA rings and cages. It involves strength and leverage that are used to move, subdue or even throw an opponent. When judo is contested at the Olympics and other sanctioned events, participants wear a gi, and grabbing an opponent's gi to assist in a throw or takedown is very common. MMA fighters in the UFC are not permitted to wear gis.

Renowned fighters like Fedor Emelianenko, Paulo Filho and Karo Parisyan credit judo as a major reason for their success.

STRATEGY

In any fighting discipline, a martial artist needs to enter his fight with a strategy. Understanding the other fighter's tendencies and weaknesses can go a long way to helping secure victory.

In MMA, any successful fighter needs to have some proficiency in at least one type of fighting that takes place on the ground, like wrestling or Brazilian jiu-jitsu, and one style of fighting that is a standup striking discipline, like boxing or kickboxing. Fights in MMA are always unpredictable, and when facing an opponent who can theoretically do anything in the ring, it benefits a fighter to be able to trade strikes as well as fend off takedowns and apply submissions. A wrestler with no ability to defend himself at all against a boxer will more than likely find himself knocked out. Conversely, a boxer without any knowledge of submission defense will not last long if a submission fighter takes him to the mat.

The fighter who is able to move the fight into the area where he has an advantage will usually win. For example, when Georges St-Pierre successfully defended his UFC welterweight belt against Nick Diaz, he turned the fight into a wrestling match and dominated for five rounds. St-Pierre is a good boxer, but so is Diaz. He knew his wrestling skills were far superior to Diaz's, so it made sense for him to use them instead of taking his chances on his feet.

An example of a fighter not using a perceived skill advantage happened in August of 2006. Renato "Babalu" Sobral made a poor strategic decision in his title match with Chuck Liddell and predictably paid the price. Despite being an excellent ground fighter — far better than Liddell — he made only one attempt to take the fight to the ground before deciding he would simply box the champion. The results were predictable, and it took Liddell only a couple of minutes to knock the Brazilian out.

RULES

There are many MMA organizations across the globe, past and current, that use essentially the same rules. The UFC is far and away the most successful and popular of the professional fighting circuits, so we'll use the rules that govern the UFC for our example. Initially the promotion marketed fights as having "no rules," and the MMA itself was often referred to as no-holds-barred (NHB) fighting. However, even back when the UFC began there were a few rules: eye gouging, fish hooking and groin strikes were all prohibited.

Today most fans are surprised to learn of just how many rules there are. Some purists deride the number of rules, but realistically, to be a professional sport in North America, "anything goes" fighting simply can't exist and be sanctioned. The rules the UFC has installed are there to

Quinton Jackson's cornermen remind him of his in-fight strategy between rounds of his light heavyweight bout against Jon Jones at UFC 135.

protect the fighters and ensure the matches are as authentic as possible. It makes for a controlled environment that keeps fighters honest and, really, saves lives.

The UFC's rules govern everything, from the size of the octagon to the number of cornermen to hand wrapping, clothing, mouthguards and footwear. But most important, they dictate what a fighter may and may not do in the ring. The following is a list of prohibited activities:

- Butting with the head
- Eye gouging of any kind
- Biting
- Spitting at an opponent
- Hair pulling
- Fish hooking
- Groin attacks of any kind
- Putting a finger into any orifice or any cut or laceration of an opponent
- Small joint manipulation
- Striking downward using the point of the elbow
- Striking to the spine or the back of the head
- Kicking to the kidney with a heel
- Throat strikes of any kind, including, without limitation, grabbing the trachea
- Clawing, pinching or twisting the flesh
- Grabbing the clavicle
- Kicking the head of a grounded opponent
- Kneeing the head of a grounded opponent
- Stomping a grounded opponent
- Holding the fence
- Holding the shorts or gloves of an opponent
- Using abusive language in the fenced ring/fighting area
- Engaging in any unsportsmanlike conduct that causes injury to an opponent
- Attacking an opponent on or during the break
- Attacking an opponent who is under the care of the referee
- Attacking an opponent after the bell has sounded the end of the round
- Timidity, including, without limitation, avoiding contact with an opponent, intentionally or consistently dropping the mouthpiece, or faking an injury
- Throwing an opponent out of the ring/fighting area
- Flagrantly disregarding the instructions of the referee
- Spiking an opponent to the canvas on his head or neck
- Interference by the corner
- Applying any foreign substance to the hair or body to gain an advantage

WEIGHT CLASSES

Weight classes, not originally a part of MMA, were introduced after the early UFC tournaments, which featured fighters of all sizes competing against each other. Introducing weight classes accomplished two things for the UFC: it helped the organization get sanctioning from the governing bodies that regulate fighting sport in the United States, and it allowed the sport to crown multiple champions. Carrying different weight classes enabled the UFC to grow, and it gave a home to fighters of all sizes.

The UFC has champions in the following weight classes: heavyweight (205 to 265 pounds), light heavyweight (185 to 205 pounds), middleweight (170 to 185 pounds), welterweight (155 to 170 pounds), lightweight (145 to 155 pounds), featherweight (135 to 145 pounds), bantamweight (125 to 135 pounds) and flyweight (under 125 pounds). On the women's side there is only the bantamweight division for fighters 135 pounds and under. The UFC and most other promotions also sometimes hold catchweight fights. A catchweight bout is one where the martial artists agree to come in at weights that fall in between the maximum limits for weight classes. For example, if a fighter who normally fights at 170 pounds wants to take on a fighter who is normally 200, the two might agree to a catchweight bout at 185 pounds to offset any size advantages for the heavier fighter.

It should be noted that weight and, more specifically, weight cutting (the act of dropping weight before weighing in) are extremely important aspects of mixed martial arts. When a fighter competes in a specific weight class, he needs to weigh in at that weight (or 1 pound over in some cases) the day before his fight to be eligible to compete in his event. This is called making weight. It's something all fighters need to do. If they don't weigh in at the right weight, they are given a set amount of time (usually an hour) to lose the necessary pounds. If they fail to do so in that extra time, then they must forfeit the bout (in the UFC, sometimes the fighter will be given the option to forfeit 20 percent of his purse — some of which will go to the other fighter — if he agrees to fight at a catchweight). Once in a while this happens, but not often, as a forfeited fight causes huge headaches for a promoter. Obviously if a fighter fails to make weight more than one time, a promoter will be extremely reluctant to use him on a card.

Generally most fighters are very good at managing their weight and can use this as a strategic advantage. For example, when Georges St-Pierre, a large welterweight, fights BJ Penn, a natural lightweight, both men will weigh in at around 170 pounds. Penn, because of his smaller frame, will achieve this fairly easily. After the weigh-in, he'll drink some fluids and eat some energy-producing food and will probably weigh around 172 or 173 pounds by fight time a day later. St-Pierre, on the other hand, because of his naturally larger body, has to essentially starve himself and dehydrate his body in order to make the welterweight limit. Once he has done

that, he'll rehydrate and eat as well. The difference is that St-Pierre will end up entering the octagon closer to his more natural weight of 185 pounds. It may sound like a lot to gain 15 pounds after weigh-in, but fighters' bodies are perfectly honed machines, and each fighter knows what his body needs in order to respond to training. At this level of competition, a larger fighter who is able to make weight, like St-Pierre, has a tremendous advantage.

MEASURING WEIGHT

Weight class comparisons in the UFC, as represented by the champion of each division.

	CAIN VELASQUEZ	JON JONES	CHRIS WEIDMAN	JOHNY HENDRICKS	ANTHONY PETTIS	JOSE ALDO	T.J. DILLASHAW	DEMETRIOUS JOHNSON	RONDA ROUSEY
HEIGHT	6'1"	6'4"	6'0"	5'9"	5'9"	5'7"	5'6"	5'3"	5'6"
WEIGHT	241 lb.	205 lb.	185 lb.	170 lb.	155 lb.	145 lb.	135 lb.	125 lb.	135 lb.
WEIGHT CLASS	Heavyweight	Light Heavyweight	Middleweight	Welterweight	Lightweight	Featherweight	Bantamweight	Flyweight	Bantamweight

Jon Jones and Glover Teixeira battle for the light heavyweight championship at UFC 172 in 2014. Jones beat Teixeira for his seventh consecutive title defense.

THE FIGHT

Put aside all the showmanship of weigh-in trash talk, entrance music, fighter entourages and so on, and a UFC bout is a pretty simple thing. When the lights come up and the bell rings, there are only a few things that really matter.

In the UFC, nontitle bouts are scheduled for three five-minute rounds. Championship bouts are made up of five five-minute rounds.

In that time, fighters try to enact their strategy and deploy their best martial arts. The goal for every fighter is to end the fight early, as it is a grueling test of will to go the distance, and it also leaves the decision of who won to the judges, of which there are three.

The only people in the ring are the two fighters and the referee. The role of the referee is to make sure fighters don't break the rules (for which they will be penalized — a reflection of which is shown in judges' scores) and to ensure the safety of both fighters. A referee will monitor cuts, consciousness and other injuries and has the ability to stop the fight if he thinks a fighter is in danger.

Fights can end in a number of different ways. The most dramatic is the knockout. A straight knockout (KO) results from a blow that renders a fighter unconscious. A technical knockout (TKO) happens after a fighter is punched or kicked and is injured to the point where he is unable to continue.

In MMA, fights are often won by submission. In this case, the fighter who is being submitted needs to verbally or physically tap out. The referee will closely monitor submission situations in case the fighter applying the submission does not hear or feel the tap out. Occasionally a fighter will not tap out while in submission, and unless he can break the submission the fight will end in a TKO, as the submission hold will render the fighter being submitted unable to continue. Fighters who are being submitted who don't tap out sometimes lose consciousness or have joints dislocated, which was the case when Ronda Rousey caught Miesha Tate in an armbar at their 2012 Strikeforce title bout.

The fight can also be stopped by the referee if he feels one fighter is unable to defend himself, or by a doctor who decides an injury is too severe for the fight to continue. A cornerman can also end the contest by throwing a towel into the ring or cage when he feels his fighter has had enough.

If none of these situations occur, the fight will go its scheduled number of rounds and require the judges' decision. Although many controversial decisions have been rendered over the years, judges are supposed to award points to the competitor who inflicts the most damage, controls the action, shows more aggression and comes closest to ending the fight via knockout or submission.

In the UFC there are multiple variations of judging results:

- Unanimous decision: when all three judges score the contest for the same fighter
- Split decision: when two judges score the contest for one fighter and one judge scores for the opponent
- Majority decision: when two judges score the contest for the same fighter and one judge scores a draw
- Unanimous draw: when all three judges score the contest a draw
- Majority draw: when two judges score the contest a draw
- Split draw: when all three judges score differently

FROM THE FIGHTERS to the promoters to the advertisers to the fans, it is everyone's wish for a good fight, and it is in everyone's best interests. On any given fight night a number of things can go wrong, but as long as the action in the ring is clean and fair, and the two fighters are left to fight for the win, MMA as a spectator sport is difficult to top in terms of pure entertainment.

Jon Jones gets high fives from the crowd as he enters the arena to defend his light heavyweight title against Alexander Gustafsson at UFC 165. Gustafsson took Jones to a decision, where the champ prevailed.

SIMPLY THE BEST

Above: Georges St-Pierre pummels Thiago Alves at UFC 100. St-Pierre won by unanimous decision. Right: St-Pierre throws a superman punch at Johny Hendricks at UFC 167. St-Pierre won the fight but vacated the belt shortly after.

TOUGHEST. STRONGEST. SMARTEST. Superstar. The superlatives know no bounds when describing Georges St-Pierre. The French-Canadian's impact has been worldwide, ushering mixed martial arts from fringe sport to mainstream event. Along the way, "Rush" has become one of the world's most dominant fighters, a multifaceted athlete with explosive wrestling power, technically superior boxing skills and a ruthless finishing touch when on the ground. He's a black belt in jiu-jitsu. A black belt in karate. A Muay Thai expert. He's not just a champion. He's an icon.

From the small town of Saint-Isidore outside of Montreal, St-Pierre grew up bullied by his peers. But everything changed when he walked into a karate school. Since then, St-Pierre has morphed into a devastating fighter inside the ring and a humble champion outside of it.

The 5-foot-11, 170-pound welterweight with a 76-inch reach made an immediate splash, winning his first seven professional fights (including two in the UFC). That earned "GSP" a title fight against welterweight stalwart Matt Hughes at UFC 50 in 2004.

Tagged as the UFC's next up and comer, St-Pierre stood toe to toe with one of his idols. Inexperience versus top-level competition humbled the French-Canadian that night, with Hughes submitting St-Pierre. But two years later in a rematch at UFC 65, an older and wiser GSP scored the TKO in the second round after dropping Hughes with a high leg kick and finishing him on the ground.

The glory was short-lived. The following year, underdog Matt Serra knocked out the French-Canadian at UFC 83. The loss would haunt St-Pierre for years, and he used the experience as his motivation, vowing never to be that unprepared again. He has not lost a fight since, and when he was awarded a rematch with Serra in 2008, he won back the welterweight title.

As he continued winning and potential suitors for his title came knocking, the stakes grew higher for GSP. He was accused of playing it safe, afraid to lose his belt. The criticism was not without merit. Inside the octagon, it looked as though he had lost some of his knockout power. Instead, he utilized a frequent jab to keep distance and opted to shoot for takedowns rather than knockout punches. His superior technical abilities were on display in every bout — he owns the record for most significant strikes in UFC history — but as far as entertainment value went, the label "boring" crept into the conversation. Despite his technical prowess, crowds still clamored for knockouts.

That's not to cheapen GSP's accomplishments. His nine title defenses are second only to middleweight legend Anderson Silva, and St-Pierre has spent more time in the octagon than any other man on the planet. Further, the flip side of his lack of knockout power illustrates how good a tactician the welterweight is. He plans his fights, knows his strengths and preys on the weaknesses of his opponents. Exciting or not, it has proven to be overwhelmingly effective, and for that reason, GSP is still the UFC's biggest star.

When St-Pierre wrecked his knee in training in 2010 and spent 18 months on the shelf, it was devastating. But time off allowed him to think, and before returning to the octagon in 2012 he said, "I'm scared." It was an honest, refreshing take on an athlete's mental state when recuperating from injury and one of the reasons St-Pierre has endeared himself to fans outside the UFC's core demographic.

His final fight to date against Johny Hendricks in 2013 was marred by controversy. Not only did many pundits believe Hendricks claimed victory at UFC 167, but St-Pierre, looking battered and bruised, offered cryptic remarks about taking an extended absence following the fight. Turns out he was serious, and several months later, GSP vacated his post as welterweight king, citing personal issues that included mental health, obsessive-compulsive disorder and insomnia. Hendricks would go on to win the vacated belt that no other man had touched for seven years, and any talk of a St-Pierre comeback will have to wait — another serious knee injury will sideline him for all of 2014.

Even on sabbatical, St-Pierre is the world's most recognizable mixed martial artist, and he's not disappearing. He's written a book called *GSP: The Way of the Fight*, starred in a major documentary about his life titled *Takedown: The DNA of GSP* and made a cameo as a villain in *Captain America: The Winter Soldier*. His lifetime record of 25-2 and reign as champion may be over, but a new chapter awaits the once-bullied kid who became the best welterweight mixed martial artist of his generation.

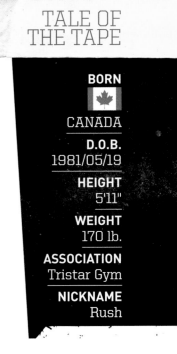

TALE OF
THE TAPE

BORN

CANADA

D.O.B.
1981/05/19

HEIGHT
5'11"

WEIGHT
170 lb.

ASSOCIATION
Tristar Gym

NICKNAME
Rush

Above: Anderson Silva defends his middleweight title against Chael Sonnen at UFC 148 in 2012. Right: Silva celebrates knocking out Yushin Okami in the UFC middleweight championship bout at UFC 134 in 2011.

TO SAY ANDERSON Silva is a titan among men is no exaggeration. Few can achieve immortality in sport, but Silva, known as "the Spider," has so thoroughly dominated during his career that the only way to do him justice is to speak in hyperbole. He is a legend, certainly a first-ballot Hall of Famer, the best middleweight fighter mixed martial arts has ever known — and perhaps the greatest pound-for-pound fighter of all time in any combat sport.

The Brazilian came from humble beginnings, raised by his aunt and uncle in Curitiba, the capital city in the province of Parana, one of the host cities of the 2014 World Cup. At 6 foot 2 and 185 pounds, Silva's body size has presented countless problems for his opponents over the years. His length, including a hard-to-counter 77.5-inch reach, keeps challengers at bay. His career statistics in the UFC are equally impressive: 78 percent takedown accuracy, 70 percent takedown defense and just 1.5 significant strikes absorbed per minute, meaning he does an excellent job of staying out of harm's way. Quite simply, he is gifted both offensively and defensively, using a varied attack to stymie opponents in the octagon. Over the course of seven years as champion, he won 16 consecutive fights, defending his title an unheard of 10 times — both UFC records.

Silva began fighting in Brazil, winning at will before making the move to Pride in Japan, where he notably dropped former UFC welterweight champion Carlos Newton with a flying knee at Pride 26 in 2003. Several years later, Silva made his UFC debut in 2006 versus Chris Leben, knocking him out in just 49 seconds to set up a title fight with Rich Franklin. The Spider disposed of Franklin in fast fashion as well, dropping the American at 2:59 of the first round at UFC 64 in October 2007. Two UFC fights and Silva owned the belt. It was that quick. He wouldn't relinquish the hardware for seven years.

But statistics don't tell the whole story — they don't describe his presence in and out of the ring, or what he means to fans and fellow fighters. "Silva does amazing things that nobody else can do," UFC president Dana White once said. "He's the greatest of all time. I think he's the greatest in any combat sport." The high praise for Silva from the head of the most influential MMA fighting loop isn't hype. Silva is one of those champions who have earned the respect of everyone who's come in contact with them — almost.

Silva's most famous fights — his rear naked choke of former Pride champion Dan Henderson at UFC 82; his embarrassment of light heavyweight champ Forrest Griffin at UFC 101; his vicious head kick to Vitor Belfort at UFC 126; his two comeback wins versus Chael Sonnen, including an improbable submission victory at UFC 117 when he appeared all but defeated — were exhibitions of his otherworldly skills. But there was also the clowning.

It began in Abu Dhabi at UFC 112 versus jiu-jitsu specialist Demian Maia. Silva taunted him all match, dropping his hands and playing mind games with the submissions expert, enticing Maia to land a punch. Silva may have escaped with the win that night, but few were

impressed with the quality of the fight, and many rolled their eyes at the lack of respect Silva showed for his opposition.

His rope-a-dope clowning became one of his calling cards, and it elevated his wins to pure spectacle. But at UFC 162, Silva finally paid for it as Chris Weidman tagged him on the chin while the star's hands were at his sides. "I think Silva is the best in the world, but he got caught," fellow superstar Georges St-Pierre said after the 2013 fight.

The rematch was memorable, but for the wrong reasons. Weidman checked a Silva kick, and the block snapped the Brazilian's shin nearly in two. The 38-year-old is sidelined until 2015, when his leg is projected to be fully healed. During his reign — 2,458 days, to be exact — Silva's dominance led to speculation of many potential superfights, including bouts against St-Pierre, Jon Jones and even boxer Roy Jones Jr. But none have materialized yet.

Silva is a legend in Brazil, and any fight with his name can generate considerable revenue. So don't expect Silva to exit quietly because of his injury. In fact, while sidelined, the Spider is training to become a Los Angeles police officer. His career record now stands at 33-6. Rest assured, whomever he fights, wherever he fights, the legendary Brazilian, soon pushing 40, will put on a show for the ages.

TALE OF THE TAPE

BORN

BRAZIL

D.O.B.
1975/04/14

HEIGHT
6'2"

WEIGHT
185 lb.

ASSOCIATION
Team
Nogueira /
X-Gym /
Killer Bees

NICKNAME
The Spider

FRANK SHAMROCK

Above: Frank Shamrock attempts to submit Yuki Kondo at the Pancrase Anniversary Show in 1996. Right: Shamrock defends his light heavyweight belt against Tito Ortiz at UFC 22 in 1999.

THE ADOPTED BROTHER of MMA pioneer Ken Shamrock, Frank Shamrock staked his own claim as a major player in the early days of Pancrase and the UFC, carving out a career that paved the way for generations to follow.

At 5 foot 10 and 185 pounds, the early trailblazer was a Pancrase legend, beginning his professional career in late 1994 at the King of Pancrase tournament versus the well-known Dutchman Bas Rutten, a major player at the time and later a well-known TV personality. Shamrock scored a victory that night, but

Rutten would become a daunting opponent during the first several years of Shamrock's career, defeating him twice.

Several other rivalries surfaced in the mid-1990s on the Pancrase circuit, including noted battles against established Japanese stars like Masakatsu Funaki and Minoru Suzuki, the pioneers of Pancrase. His second win versus Suzuki was formidable — at 22:53 of the bout, he finally submitted Suzuki with a kneebar to win the interim title. In all, Shamrock scrapped 18 times for the promotion, notching 11 wins before leaving for greener pastures.

He reeled off wins in the RINGS promotion as well as the 1997 Pankration World Championship, where he barely defeated tough-as-nails Enson Inoue in what Shamrock later called the toughest fight of his career. "There was a time during that fight where I thought I might lose and die in the ring," Shamrock said in 2003.

He survived, landing in the UFC several months later. It took just 16 seconds to establish himself as the man to beat, submitting Kevin Jackson for the light heavyweight title in late 1997, a UFC record for fastest submission in a title bout. Five more fights followed without a loss, his final UFC victory an exclamation point of his dominance.

Tito Ortiz was making a name for himself at the turn of the century. Shamrock already had one. But he had a point to prove versus Ortiz, who'd picked a fight with the Lion's Den, the training camp run by Frank's brother, Ken. Mess with one Shamrock and you mess with them all — or at least that's how the UFC sold it. Although the adopted brothers both became MMA stars, with the elder Ken even training Frank early on in his career, the two had grown apart. Despite this, the UFC hyped the fight as Ortiz versus the Shamrocks.

In September 1999, Frank stood facing Ortiz in Lake Charles, Louisiana, at UFC 22. Ortiz outweighed Shamrock considerably, and starting strong, he dominated the fight with takedowns and subsequent shots on the ground. But Shamrock weathered the storm and, with better cardio, waited until Ortiz gassed out in the fourth round to strike. Hammerfists followed, and Ortiz tapped out at 4:42.

Shamrock semiretired shortly thereafter, fighting just twice in the next six years, winning the World Extreme Cagefighting light heavyweight belt in 2003 against Bryan Pardoe and then fighting Cesar Gracie at a Strikeforce event in 2006 — the first MMA event sanctioned in California. Entering the Gracie bout, Shamrock hadn't lost since 1997, riding an 11-fight unbeaten streak. Gracie was 40, had never fought an MMA bout and

was primarily a Brazilian jiu-jitsu instructor whose students included future UFC stars Nick and Nate Diaz. Twenty seconds into their mismatch, Shamrock would make it 12 in a row without a loss when he knocked out Gracie, the fastest in Strikeforce history.

A year later Shamrock stepped into the ring versus Renzo Gracie at an EliteXC: Destiny event, but this time he wouldn't get the win as he was disqualified for illegal knee shots. When he choked out Phil Baroni several months later to capture the Strikeforce middleweight title — Baroni refused to tap and was rendered unconscious for a short time — Shamrock could lay claim to being a belt holder in four separate organizations. It would be the final victory of his long and varied career, however. A loss to Cung Le, who broke Shamrock's arm with a kick in the third round of their 2008 fight, ended Shamrock's brief Strikeforce reign. His final opponent, Nick Diaz — avenging his coach Cesar Gracie's loss two years prior — ushered Shamrock out of the ring for good.

Shamrock hasn't left the sport altogether. He's written an autobiography, has coached a reality series and runs several MMA academies. Retiring with a record of 23-10-2, the MMA star wasn't just the second most famous Shamrock — he was a decorated fighter in his own right who ensured a global legacy in the sport of MMA.

TALE OF THE TAPE

BORN

🇺🇸

UNITED STATES

D.O.B.
1972/12/08

HEIGHT
5'10"

WEIGHT
185 lb.

ASSOCIATION
The Alliance

NICKNAME
N/A

BJ PENN

Above: BJ Penn submits Kenny Florian with a rear naked choke at 3:54 of the fourth round at UFC 101 to defend his light heavyweight title. Right: BJ Penn applies an armbar to Jens Pulver during *The Ultimate Fighter* season 5 finale.

IT'S NO WONDER BJ Penn became known as "the Prodigy." One of the fastest men ever to earn a black belt in Brazilian jiu-jitsu, and the first non-native Brazilian to finish in first place in the World Jiu-Jitsu Championship, the Hawaiian mixed martial artist landed on the mainland with a bang, and in the process he became one of the greatest MMA stars of his generation.

Born in Honolulu to an Irish father from Kansas and a Korean-Hawaiian mother, Penn's family moved to the Big Island of Hawaii when he was 4 years old, settling in the largest town on the east coast, Hilo. Penn's given name is Jay Dee Penn — the same as his father and several of his brothers — but in the Penn clan, the second youngest boy became known as "Baby Jay," or "BJ."

His record of 16-10-2 belies the importance he's had on the rise of MMA. Penn ushered in the lightweight division, proving that smaller weight classes could be just as entertaining as watching the big boys swing. He's fought in four distinct weight classes and held titles in two divisions at the same time. Tough yet likeable, fiercely competitive and always entertaining in the octagon thanks to a top-level submission game and technical boxing skills, Penn was the perfect face for a growing sport seeking legitimacy from the mainstream.

If one fight defined Penn's early years, it was in 2004 versus Matt Hughes at UFC 46. Until then, Penn had been scrapping at 155 pounds but moved up to welterweight to fight Hughes, who had all but cleaned out the 170-pound division, defending his title five times until the nasty Hawaiian showed up that late January night in Vegas. Hughes, riding a 13-fight winning streak, was cocky before the bout, claiming he could "break [Penn] in the first round." Those words would come back to haunt him — Penn took the fight to the mat early and never relented, submitting Hughes at 4:39 by rear naked choke, an upset that shocked the world. Extremely emotional after the fight, Penn said, "To be the best, you gotta be one crazy son of a bitch."

He left the UFC for two years (some say for a bigger payday), fighting in K-1 and going 3-1, with his only loss coming against Lyoto Machida, whom Penn tangled with in a catchweight contest, Penn at 191 pounds and Machida at 220 pounds. Upon his return, Penn was streaky and incurred several notable losses, including twice to Georges St-Pierre — UFC 58 and 94 — the latter a title shot in which he failed to wrestle the belt away from the French-Canadian. Both men were in their prime, but fighting a larger welterweight like St-Pierre took its toll on Penn. The Hawaiian ate a superman punch in the third round and was never the same — St-Pierre took advantage, swarming Penn and pounding relentlessly on the weakened fighter, who quit after the fourth round on advice from his cornermen. The match wasn't without controversy — Penn's camp accused the French-Canadian of "greasing," or adding Vaseline to his body in between rounds, but it was never proven.

Penn returned to lightweight and defended his 155-pound belt twice, choking out Kenny Florian and finishing Diego Sanchez via TKO.

But his run as a dominant force was nearing its end when he met fast punching Frankie Edgar in 2010. Penn lost both the title fight and the rematch. Some might be devastated; instead, Penn rose back up to 170 pounds to meet his old foe Hughes, whom he sent packing in just 21 seconds. It was the last win of his career.

When Edgar and Penn faced each other for the third and final time at the conclusion of The Ultimate Fighter 19 in 2014, Penn was coming off a loss to Rory MacDonald in which he looked more punching bag than pro fighter. His lopsided loss to Edgar further proved age had finally caught up with the legend.

"This is the end," Penn said post fight. "My biggest regret would have been if I didn't get in the ring . . . I would have always wondered [if I could still fight] . . . Now I know for sure."

In Hilo, Penn Training and Fitness Center now stands as a testament to the Prodigy and a place for the Hawaiian to give back to a new generation of fighters. He's guaranteed a spot in the UFC Hall of Fame as a trailblazer, icon and flag bearer for a sport that needed heroes as it emerged from obscurity.

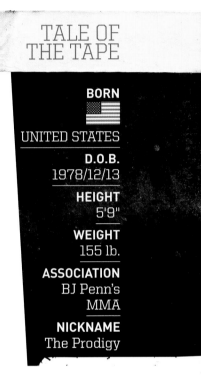

TALE OF THE TAPE

BORN
🇺🇸
UNITED STATES
D.O.B.
1978/12/13
HEIGHT
5'9"
WEIGHT
155 lb.
ASSOCIATION
BJ Penn's MMA
NICKNAME
The Prodigy

DAN HENDERSON

Above: Dan Henderson readies himself for battle against Mauricio "Shogun" Rua at UFC 139. Henderson scored a unanimous decision over the heavy-hitting Rua. Right: Henderson lands a wicked right on Rafael "Feijao" Cavalcante at Strikeforce: Feijao vs. Henderson, in 2011.

THE FACT DAN Henderson is still fighting at 43 years old is a victory in itself. But look beyond the curtain of longevity and a storied career emerges, one that's spanned three decades and taken the California native from Strikeforce to Pride to the UFC. Along the way, he's amassed a 30-12 record fighting in nearly every conceivable weight class, from the 170-pound welterweight division all the way to heavyweight. He's the only man to hold two titles concurrently in two divisions. He's a two-time Pride champion and two-time Olympian.

He's a surefire Hall of Famer, but to his fans, he's just "Hendo."

Square-jawed and cauliflower-eared, if anyone has the look of an MMA superhero, it's Henderson, who at age 20 qualified for the 1992 Summer Olympics. He'd skyrocketed from second-best high school wrestler in the state of California to tops in the country. Former heavyweight belt holder Randy Couture once said, "Danny's got a high tolerance for pain." Another fighter, Nate Quarry, likened Henderson's musculature to "steel cable."

Possessing a deceivingly compact 71-inch

reach, the stout 5-foot-11 American has scrapped nearly every legendary fighter of the last 15 years. But it was in Japan where Henderson really cut his teeth, competing in three divisions over the course of a storied Pride career. His rivalry there with Wanderlei Silva was the stuff Hall of Fame careers are built on. Henderson lost his Pride debut to the Brazilian, but he avenged the defeat six years later, beating Silva to capture the middleweight title. He already owned the welterweight belt, and the win made him the first man in MMA to reign over two weight classes simultaneously.

But UFC 100 topped it all. The centennial featured several of the biggest names in the sport. Brock Lesnar and Georges St-Pierre both put their belts up, and even a young Jon Jones — the future light heavyweight champ — fought in the preliminaries. But no one made more waves that night than Henderson and British fighter Michael Bisping. After jawing at each other during season 9 of *The Ultimate Fighter*, the two coaches squared off as the top two contenders for the middleweight crown. Henderson said before the fight, "I'll have my chance to shut his mouth with my fist." And that's exactly what he did. Loading up his powerful right hand, known as "the H Bomb," Henderson caught Bisping and mercilessly knocked out the Brit at 3:20 of the second round. For many, it was the knockout of the year.

For Hendo, it capped off three straight wins. And yet, instead of riding the wave, he fell off the board. Contract negotiations fell through with the UFC. Then, a loss to Jake Shields in the Strikeforce middleweight title bout embarrassed him after he signed a four-fight deal with the organization. Maybe he was angry, but after the Shields loss, Henderson rattled off three wins at light heavyweight, then put on extra pounds and moved up to heavyweight to fight MMA legend Fedor Emelianenko. The Russian, who at one point was undefeated in Pride for 10 years, was promptly disposed of with a vicious uppercut to the chin.

For recent fight fans, it's Henderson's skirmishes with Mauricio "Shogun" Rua that will be remembered as the pinnacle of an outstanding career. No one expected such fireworks when the two met in late 2011. The aging scrappers did not disappoint in their five-round nontitle fight at UFC 139. Henderson outhit the Brazilian early, outlanding him 106-66 in the punch department. But something stirred in Shogun and he found another gear. "That guy can take a punch," Henderson said later. And he could give them, too, dominating the fifth round by a 79-9 count. But Henderson was simply too much early on and took the decision. It's been called one of the greatest fights in MMA history.

They met again in 2014 at UFC Fight Night 38, and despite being outclassed for the first two rounds, Hendo capitalized on a poor clinch from Rua in the third and sent the Brazilian flying backward with a thunderous right, breaking his nose and ending the bout. "This one means more than most," Henderson said following the fight. In his most recent bout, however, Henderson succumbed to a Daniel Cormier submission at UFC 173, refusing to tap out in what could be a final act of obstinance from the legendary competitor.

The wrestler with the iron chin and super powerful punch has a resume worthy of the UFC Hall of Fame. It's just a matter of when he'll get the call.

TALE OF THE TAPE

BORN

🇺🇸

UNITED STATES

D.O.B.
1970/08/24

HEIGHT
5'11"

WEIGHT
205 lb.

ASSOCIATION
Team Quest

NICKNAME
Hendo

FEDOR EMELIANENKO

Above and right: Fedor Emelianenko tangles with Dan Henderson at Strikeforce: Fedor vs. Henderson. The bout was only Fedor's fourth loss of his MMA career, which featured 34 victories over 12 years.

FOR ALL THE hype in fighting, there are few who live up to it and stand as true living legends. Fedor Emelianenko is one of those men who have, and for some, he is the beginning and end of the conversation when it comes to "the greatest ever." Despite never having fought in the UFC, the Russian will go down as one of the best heavyweight mixed martial artists the world has ever seen, if not the best.

Trained in judo, sambo and jiu-jitsu, his list of accomplishments is lengthy: He has carried three heavyweight titles in three different promotions. He posted 10 knockout wins and 16 submission wins and went undefeated in 28 fights, spanning nearly a decade. Sporting a 34-4-1-lifetime record, "the Last Emperor" was quite simply unstoppable for the majority of his career. But the "baddest man on the planet," according to one writer, wasn't that imposing. At 6 feet and 230 pounds, he often fought men much larger than himself. But utilizing a dizzying array of striking and submission skills, the Russian went on to a decorated MMA career that's unrivaled.

Raised in the small Russian mining town

of Stary Oskol, 400 miles north of Moscow, Emelianenko's humble beginnings permeated throughout his life and career. Serving in the Russian army during the mid-1990s, Emelianenko trained in martial arts during his time off, and upon finishing his military stint, he won national championships in both sambo and judo. He began his MMA career in the Japanese organization RINGS, where he went 10-1 over a two-year period, the only defeat a controversial doctor stoppage.

Known for a lack of ceremony when entering an arena, his first Pride bout, against heavyweight Semmy Schilt, was memorable mostly for the height difference. Schilt stood nearly 7 feet tall, but the Russian cut him down to size, working a ground and pound he'd become famous for. It was his first of 15 bouts in Pride without a loss.

His trilogy of fights with fellow heavyweight Antonio Rodrigo Nogueira began in 2003. The Brazilian was a heavy favorite at Pride 25, the most well-rounded and dangerous heavyweight in the organization. The night featured a host of huge names: Dan Henderson, Rampage Jackson, Anderson Silva. When it was all over, the biggest one of all was Fedor, who dared to enter Nogueira's renowned guard, avoiding submission attempts and pounding away at will. Announcer Stephen Quadros described the scene that evening as "somebody hitting a buffalo with a baseball bat." The Russian would be rewarded with the heavyweight title.

The following year, he submitted former UFC heavyweight champ Kevin Randleman, despite the American's overhead suplex of Emelianenko that nearly ended the fight with a thunderous blow. The Russian miraculously recovered, winning by kimura.

But perhaps the pinnacle of Fedor's legendary career occurred August 28, 2005, versus Mirko "Cro Cop" Filipovic. A crowd of 47,000-plus gathered in Saitama, Japan, to witness the event. Despite suffering a broken nose at the hands of the Croatian kickboxing specialist, who hadn't lost in seven fights, the Russian soldiered on. Closing distance and

initiating clinches in tight, Emelianenko was able to take down Cro Cop and employ his patented ground and pound. The win put an exclamation point on an already savage run, as Fedor was able to avenge a loss his brother, Alexander, had suffered at the hands of Filipovic one year earlier.

During the next several years, Emelianenko ended five consecutive fights by tapout. When he choked out 6-foot-8 former UFC belt holder Tim Sylvia in just 36 seconds, Sylvia remarked, "I was amazed at how good he is. The guy's a stud. I don't think he's human."

Why Emelianenko never fought in the UFC is up for debate. UFC president Dana White blamed the fighter's management company, M-1 Global, for mismanaging their superstar, who signed instead with Strikeforce in 2010. But the Russian's better days were behind him. When Brazilian Fabricio Werdum forced Emelianenko to tap out, it sent shockwaves around the world. The baddest man on the planet had been broken. The unbeaten streak was over. Two more fighters would best him, and although Emelianenko finished his career with three more wins, they were pedestrian in nature. He retired in 2012 after 39 professional MMA fights.

For a generation of fans, Fedor is the ultimate fighter. A lack of pretense and an extraordinary range of skills made him a people's man and a fighter's fighter who dominated the global MMA landscape. When discussing the heavyweight class, he may be the beginning of the conversation. He may be the end. Probably both.

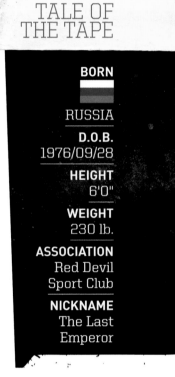

TALE OF THE TAPE

BORN

RUSSIA

D.O.B.
1976/09/28

HEIGHT
6'0"

WEIGHT
230 lb.

ASSOCIATION
Red Devil
Sport Club

NICKNAME
The Last
Emperor

JON JONES

Above: Jon Jones kicks Ryan Bader during their light heavyweight bout at UFC 126. Jones won the fight and went on to take the light heavyweight title in his next bout. Right: Jones defeats Brandon Vera by TKO in the first round at UFC Live 1.

THERE HAS NEVER been anyone like Jon Jones. No one has been so good so fast, and no one has been so athletically gifted and so impossible to beat. At the rate he is going, Jones has the potential to become the Michael Jordan or Wayne Gretzky of MMA — the most dominant player of all time.

Jones was born in Endicott, New York, into a family of athletes. His father, an all-city wrestler who became a Pentecostal pastor, passed along his love for the sport to his three sons. Jones admittedly didn't excel at conventional sports — he was so skinny his high school football teammates nicknamed him "Bones" — and he has trouble dunking a basketball, even at 6 foot 4. But wrestling ran in his blood, and hours spent grappling with his two massive brothers, who have both become defensive linemen in the NFL, prepared him well for the rigors of combat.

As the junior national champion at Iowa Central Community College, Jones spent several years wrestling before returning home to Rochester to be with his expecting girlfriend in 2007. He began training at a local MMA gym on a whim, and just one year later entered the ring. He was a natural, and within four months, Jones had posted a 6-0 record, including a 14-second knockout. Sporting an 84.5-inch reach — the longest in the UFC — Jones made his debut with the promotion at UFC 87.

His ability to throw gravity-defying spinning elbows and flying knees made him an instant attraction, and after defeating Andre Gusmao by decision he dusted veteran Stephan Bonnar. That made UFC president Dana White sit up and take notice. "This kid is tough," he thought at the time. And he's not only physically tough. The former choir singer is a spiritual warrior, quoting Tony Robbins and taking the martial arts side of MMA seriously, incorporating meditation into his training. He has Philippians 4:13 tattooed on his chest to honor his sister, Carmen, who died of brain cancer at just 17 years old.

That mental fortitude translated in the octagon. In 2011, after three consecutive finishes over Brandon Vera, Vladimir Matyushenko and Ryan Bader, Jones landed a shot at the UFC light heavyweight title. At 23, he became the youngest person to ever win a UFC belt when he defeated Mauricio "Shogun" Rua at UFC 128 in 2011. He has not relinquished the belt since, owning a professional record that now stands at 20-1, which includes the greatest takedown defense of all time in the UFC at 97 percent and top-10 standing in significant strikes landed, just below legends BJ Penn and Georges St-Pierre.

With his lethal mix of intelligence and athleticism, Jones has since cleaned out the 205-pound division, defeating four former champions along the way: Quinton "Rampage" Jackson, Lyoto Machida, Rashad Evans and Vitor Belfort.

His toughest fight to date came in late 2013 versus Alexander Gustafsson. Battling for five rounds at UFC 165, both men sustained considerable damage and spent the night in hospital. The bout was named Fight of the Night and later Fight of the Year for 2013. Former light heavyweight champ Tito Ortiz, who once held the most title defenses in the division, said in 2013, "I don't think there's anybody in this sport right now with the technique and skills that he has." Jones has since eclipsed Ortiz's record.

Jones' most recent bout at UFC 172 versus Glover Teixeira — previously undefeated in 20 fights — was an absolute clinic for Jones, as he methodically picked the challenger apart with a mix of creative choices. He used in-close elbows, hooks and jabs for a total significant strike percentage of 58 percent, and he landed 138 hard blows alone. "It was a lot of improv," he said after the fight. He even utilized a standing shoulder lock to wrench Teixeira's arm early in the bout, causing considerable pain. The Brazilian never recovered. Jones has now defended his title seven times, sporting an 11-fight winning streak. If it continues, he'll shatter middleweight Anderson Silva's UFC records for consecutive victories (16) and title defenses (10).

Jones' success, looks and likeability have endeared him to marketers. Nike created Bones Knows, which includes footwear and apparel, and Jones is now worth millions on top of his fighting pay.

Some have called him the Muhammad Ali of MMA. He has never been submitted. Never been knocked out. Never lost by decision. When his career is over, Jon "Bones" Jones will go down as one of the greatest pound-for-pound fighters ever to enter the octagon. Until then, sit back and enjoy the ride.

TALE OF THE TAPE

BORN

UNITED STATES

D.O.B.
1987/07/19

HEIGHT
6'4"

WEIGHT
205 lb.

ASSOCIATION
Jackson-Wink MMA

NICKNAME
Bones

LYOTO MACHIDA

Above: Lyoto Machida lands a devastating front kick to knock out Randy Couture and win their light heavyweight bout at UFC 129 in 2011. Right: Machida kicks Gegard Mousasi at UFC Fight Night: Machida vs. Mousasi in 2014. Machida won the middleweight match by unanimous decision.

PERHAPS NO FIGHTER on the planet exemplifies how far mixed martial arts has come over the centuries. A Brazilian of Japanese heritage, Lyoto Machida, the son of a karate master, merged the ancient art with modern jiu-jitsu to become one of the most dangerous mixed martial artists of his generation.

His father Yoshizo arrived in Brazil at 22 years old with two sets of clothes and nonexistent Portuguese. But his enthusiasm for karate translated into a teaching job at a martial arts academy. Lyoto was by far the prodigy of his four brothers. Rising to black belt in karate by 13, "the Dragon" was set for the international stage and big competition. In just his third professional fight, the 6-foot-1 fighter with the 74-inch reach handed future UFC middleweight champion Rich Franklin his first professional loss, establishing himself as someone to watch. He took on BJ Penn — who'd disposed of Matt Hughes one year earlier to claim the UFC's welterweight crown — in Japan in 2005, defeating the Hawaiian in a catchweight bout for the short-lived K-1 Hero's promotion, proving he could defeat top competition.

Machida was 8-0 by the time he reached the UFC, and he reeled off another six consecutive wins using a counterpunch, defense-first style to earn himself a light heavyweight title shot. At the time, a merry-go-round in the division saw the belt switch hands several times over the course of several years. Machida snatched it at UFC 98 from Rashad Evans, who'd upset Forrest Griffin six months prior in late 2008. The UFC's matchmaker, Joe Silva, then pitted Brazilian versus Brazilian, matching Machida and Mauricio "Shogun" Rua, the former Pride light heavyweight champion.

Shogun took it to Machida, and their five-round bout was a thriller. It went to the judges, with Machida emerging victorious and defending his title. The UFC immediately scheduled a rematch, and in 2010, Rua served notice that he deserved to beat Machida the first time, knocking out the champ before the first round was out, and the division once again had a new victor.

Machida then produced one of the greatest knockouts of all time, channeling Ralph Macchio in *The Karate Kid* to drop legend Randy Couture with a crane kick in 2011 at UFC 129 in Toronto. Coming off a pair of losses, it signaled Machida was back in the hunt, and the UFC gave the Brazilian another shot at the light heavyweight title versus phenom Jon Jones, who had disposed of Rua in 2011.

The son of the karate master was no match for Jones. Despite a first round that saw Machida create havoc with his defensive southpaw stance, even landing a small flurry of punches off the counter, Jones worked to lock Machida in a standing guillotine choke that ended the fight at 4:26 of the second round. "He's just smart," Jones said after the bout. "He kicked really hard. He knows his range. He was a challenge." His next three fights were unmemorable, as if the run at another title shot had tired Machida. Worse than wins and losses during this time, his bouts against Ryan Bader, Dan Henderson and Phil Davis were barely watchable, and Machida moved down to middleweight to compete against new competition.

The transition invigorated him. The thing about Machida is that he's always in the mix. Moving down to 185 pounds, he finished Mark Munoz with a destructive head kick, then dominated Gegard Mousasi, proving he was well above the middling middleweight competition to earn a 2014 title fight against Chris Weidman, the man who dethroned the indomitable Anderson Silva.

Machida is revered in Brazil and a top pay-per-view draw globally. Despite criticism regarding his fighting style owing to his defensive posturing, he provides an interesting style matchup versus opponents. The Brazilian still talks of another crack at Jones, revealing to broadcaster Jon Anik in 2014 that he wants a superfight between the two. But the likelihood of that fight happening anytime soon took a hit when Machida failed to knock off Chris Weidman at 185 pounds in their duel at UFC 175 — a match Weidman won by unanimous decision. What is clear for Machida is that at 35 years old and sporting a 24-5 lifetime record, the Brazilian is showing no signs of slowing down. He looked good against Weidman despite taking the loss, and he'll be in the mix for a while yet. He still wants to be a champion, so, if there is anyone the front-runners of the middleweight class shouldn't count out, it's the karate kid.

TALE OF THE TAPE

BORN
BRAZIL

D.O.B.
1978/05/30

HEIGHT
6'1"

WEIGHT
185 lb.

ASSOCIATION
APAM / Team Machida

NICKNAME
The Dragon

Above: Jose Aldo takes it to the "Korean Zombie," Chan Sung Jung, as he defends his featherweight title at UFC 163. Right: Aldo defeats Ricardo Lamas in their featherweight championship fight at UFC 169.

BRAZIL IS FAR enough to feel a world away. But growing up in Manaus, the largest city in Amazonas and gateway to the mighty South American river, is another thing altogether. There are no roads linking the jungle city to the coast. The air is thick and hot. This is where featherweight Jose Aldo was born. This is where he left, at 17, to train in Rio de Janeiro. The boy from the jungle turned out to be one of the most complete mixed martial artists the world has ever seen.

Ten years later, at just 27, it feels as if the 5-foot-7 featherweight champion has been around forever. He hasn't lost a bout since Jungle Fight 5 took place in his hometown in 2005. After 17 consecutive wins, Aldo, a jiu-jitsu black belt, is the undisputed champion at 145 pounds, the class of the featherweight division. So much so he plans on abdicating the crown and moving up 10 pounds to compete in the lightweight division. That's how good he is: there's no one left to beat.

He attacks his opponents from different angles — hard striking, swift moving and lethal on the ground. This, combined with impeccable defense — he owns one of the highest takedown defense percentages in UFC history (92 percent) and a significant strike defense at 74 percent, good enough to crack the top 10 — is what makes Aldo so dangerous. His seven-second win versus Cub Swanson — one seriously tough customer — goes down as arguably the greatest and most thrilling stoppage the MMA world has ever seen. The Brazilian's double flying knee to Swanson's head was so creative and explosive that it sent shockwaves throughout the Sacramento arena that night. The moment revealed everything that Aldo's about: speed, power, precision, even a sense of ruthlessness. As Swanson lay bloodied and stunned on the mat, Aldo cruised around the ring, dancing and pounding his chest, the complete opposite of the calm man who just seconds earlier stood in the ring with his head bowed, lethal even in his preparation.

Before World Extreme Cagefighting folded into the UFC, Aldo knocked out Mike Brown in late 2009 to become the 145-pound champ. He defended the WEC belt twice, first defeating Urijah Faber at WEC 48 in a five-round contest, then stopping Manvel Gamburyan in the second round five months later in the fall of 2010. His UFC debut the following year is one of the most memorable fights of his career, and one Canadian fans won't soon forget. Mark Hominick, Canada's pride and joy at featherweight, was riding a five-fight winning streak, including four finishes.

A crowd of 55,000 people filled the Rogers Centre in Toronto that night, making UFC 129 the biggest stage either Hominick or Aldo had ever fought on. The Brazilian dominated the bout early on, employing his patented, painful leg kicks to inflict early damage on the Canadian and gaining position on the ground, where he dropped elbow after elbow on Hominick's head. Punches flew both ways for the next couple of rounds. Aldo finally connected with a big right in the fourth. Hominick's forehead began swelling and a hematoma formed, "the size of a baseball" according to one writer after the fight. But

the plucky, undeterred Canuck soldiered on, and in the fifth, despite the gruesome-looking injury, Hominick put Aldo on the ground in a show of resilience. It wasn't enough. Both men were awarded bonuses for the performance, and Aldo said following the match: "Take your hat off in congratulations to Mark Hominick. He's a hell of a fighter."

Since Hominick, Aldo's been unstoppable. Formidable names like Kenny Florian, Chad Mendes and Frankie Edgar have all taken a shot — all have fallen at the hands of the mighty Brazilian whose lifetime record now stands at 24-1, with 14 KOs. He's currently second on the UFC's pound-for-pound best fighters list. However, he's been criticized for playing it safe lately, being less aggressive than he used to be, and perhaps that's why the 27-year-old is moving up to lightweight. He needs a challenge. He needs someone with the same skill set to compete against. Someone like Anthony Pettis, who has lobbied for a superfight with Aldo.

It's the fight everyone wants to see. Two of the fastest, most explosively gifted mixed martial artists testing their mettle versus one another for the lightweight belt. For Aldo, a win would put him with a select class of men who have held titles in two different weight classes, which might be the new sign of an ultimate champion.

TALE OF THE TAPE

BORN

BRAZIL

D.O.B.
1986/09/09

HEIGHT
5'7"

WEIGHT
145 lb.

ASSOCIATION
Nova Uniao

NICKNAME
Scarface

Above: Renan Barao pounds Urijah Faber as he defends his bantamweight title at UFC 169. Right: Barao knocks out Eddie Wineland with a kick to the head in their UFC interim bantamweight title fight at UFC 165.

FOR FIVE YEARS, the people of Brazil knew his greatness. From his hometown of Natal to Rio de Janeiro to Sao Paolo, Barao rattled off win after win from 2005 to 2010. By the time he reached North America to join the World Extreme Cagefighting promotion, he'd amassed a 23-1-1 record, the only blemishes a loss he suffered in his first professional bout and a fight scored no contest for an illegal soccer kick to the head. Until 2014, the Brazilian held one of the longest winning records in MMA history, 33 straight without a loss, and he should be a stalwart in the 135-pound class for years to come.

The bantamweight brawler with a black belt in jiu-jitsu didn't disappoint in his North American debut, defeating the WEC's Anthony Leone at a catchweight of 142 pounds in Edmonton, Alberta, submitting him by armbar in the third round. The WEC was bought by the UFC in early 2011, and Barao immediately found himself fighting for the largest promotion in the world. He subsequently knocked off wily UFC veterans Brad Pickett and Scott Jorgensen, turning heads in the process. But as the maxim goes, to be good you need to be lucky, and luck was on Barao's side when Dominick Cruz, the UFC bantamweight champion, tore his ACL in May 2012.

Cruz's absence opened up the division, and in just his fourth fight in the UFC, Barao stood across from the biggest name he'd ever faced: Urijah Faber. The two squared off for the interim bantamweight title, Barao's first five-round contest in the UFC. He didn't disappoint. Using a strategy similar to one employed by fellow Brazilian Jose Aldo — whom Faber fought earlier for the feather-weight title — Barao used swift kicks to keep the notoriously in shape Faber at a distance. In the fourth round alone he attempted 67 significant strikes, landing 21 for a solid 31 percent in the waning rounds. "I knew Faber was a great fighter," Barao said afterward. "But I came well prepared and I executed my strategy." Faber simply couldn't get inside to mount an attack and use his wrestling skills. "Those kicks were coming from pretty far out," Faber acknowledged.

Barao didn't stop there. The Brazilian defended the interim title against a much younger Michael McDonald at UFC on Fuel TV 7 in 2013, stopping the rising American star in the fourth round by submission with an impressive arm triangle. McDonald had come out firing, landing several punches that stunned the Brazilian. But Barao possesses a multitude of tools, and using kicks and take-downs he stuffed McDonald's early onslaught, outstriking the younger fighter 112-92 overall. In the fourth round, with McDonald's energy fading, Barao pounced and mounted his opponent, locking in the choke for the tapout.

While the UFC waited for Cruz to return so they could unify the belt, Barao faced off against another challenger, this time the tough, tattooed Eddie Wineland at UFC 165 in Toronto. Wineland had also defeated Jorgensen and Pickett en route to a title shot, and the challenger was admirable in the first round. But Barao scored one of the more get-off-the-couch knockouts in recent

memory when his spinning back kick in the second round landed square on Wineland's jaw, just the third time in UFC history such a kick has ended in a stoppage. "Barao is one of the best in the world," Wineland said after the loss. "He's a beast."

At just 27 years old, yet already a wizened veteran, Barao took on Faber once again in early 2014 after Cruz tore his groin, effectively ending his title reign. Barao and Faber scrapped for the real belt that night, and once again the Brazilian, who sports a career 96 percent takedown defense and averages 3.5 significant strikes per minute in the UFC, was simply too much to handle. He ended the fight early with his fists in the second round. The night was not without controversy, as some felt the referee ended the fight too early. In a sport that marvels over a combination of skill and fast finishes, Barao proved he possesses both in large quantities.

Though Barao was upset by the unheralded T.J. Dillashaw at UFC 173 — the Brazilian's first defeat in nearly a decade — the world can expect more of the same from Barao when he challenges for the belt in the future: spinning back kicks, crisp striking, incredible pace, strong jiu-jitsu and thrilling finishes.

TALE OF
THE TAPE

BORN
BRAZIL

D.O.B.
1987/02/27

HEIGHT
5'7"

WEIGHT
135 lb.

ASSOCIATION
Nova Uniao

NICKNAME
N/A

CHRIS WEIDMAN

Above: Chris Weidman drops an elbow on Anderson Silva at UFC 168 – a rematch of their title bout at UFC 162. Weidman defended his title. Right: Weidman kicks Demian Maia en route to victory at UFC on Fox 2 in 2012.

HERE'S HOW YOU make a name for yourself: knock out the UFC's longest-serving champion. That's exactly what Chris Weidman did to Anderson Silva in 2013 to steal away the middleweight belt from one of the greatest mixed martial artists in the world. It vaulted Weidman from just another top contender to the man to beat. And as he enters the prime of his career, his best years are yet to come.

Weidman's knockout win was a far cry from his early days. Born in Baldwin, New York, the college wrestler was a two-time All-American at Hofstra University, racking up wins versus

future UFC light heavyweights Ryan Bader and Phil Davis on the wrestling circuit. But he had no formal training in mixed martial arts until he began working with former welterweight champion Matt Serra — the man who knocked out Georges St-Pierre — at the academy Serra co-owned with his brother.

From there Weidman began studying with Ray Longo, who would become the future champ's full-time coach. "Weidman is probably the quickest study I ever taught," Longo said. And it didn't take long for the man nicknamed "the All-American" to add a brown belt in jiu-jitsu and well-rounded striking to his attack. In 2009, he entered his first professional fight, submitting his opponent in the opening round. Weidman then disposed of two more men, including future UFC middleweight Uriah Hall, both by strikes in the first round. Just two years after stepping into the cage, the quick study and All-American made his UFC debut.

The first round of his debut fight against Alessio Sakara was a steep learning curve for Weidman, as the rookie fell behind quickly. But with Serra barking orders in his corner, Weidman turned up the intensity, going five for five in takedown attempts and landing 84 punches to Sakara's 22 in the following two rounds to secure his first UFC win. In Vancouver several months later, the All-American made waves in front of the Canadian crowd at UFC 131 when he choked out Jesse Bongfeldt with a standing guillotine for submission of the night.

On the rise, Weidman showed no signs of slowing down when given tougher, big-name competition. His wins came from all facets of his game. He choked out brash-talking showman Tom Lawlor. He went the distance with top-10 contender and jiu-jitsu master Demian Maia. He ended Mark Munoz's evening at 1:37 of the second round of their 2012 bout, earning Knockout of the Night for his brutal finish on the ground with punches and elbows to Munoz's head. It was all leading up to the biggest moment of Weidman's life.

Anderson Silva had held the middleweight belt for more than seven years. He hadn't lost in 17 fights before stepping into the octagon with Weidman in 2013 at UFC 162, a fight Weidman had been begging for. It appeared Silva hadn't taken the incumbent too seriously, clowning in front of the challenger, dropping his hands to entice a punch. It was a strategy that backfired. Weidman clipped the champ, knocking him out. The reign was over. Weidman had knocked off the big whale of the MMA world.

Six months later: UFC 168, the Weidman–Silva rematch. Also known as the checked

kick heard around the world. Weidman dominated the Brazilian once again in the first round. But no one could have ever predicted what would happen in the second round. The Spider's leg snapped when it struck Weidman's knee, and an audible gasp could be heard throughout the arena that night. Weidman would call the block intentional, and Longo later referred to the move as a destruction, an old martial arts maneuver favored by Thai fighters. "One of the adjustments we made from the first fight is 'let's start checking leg kicks,'" Longo said after the fight. It was gruesome, and the broken leg has Silva sidelined until 2015. Regardless, it went down in the books as Weidman's first title defense and second win versus the skilled Brazilian. His record now stands at 11-0.

His next title defense was at UFC 175 against former light heavyweight champion Lyoto Machida. Weidman dominated the crafty karate specialist early on. Machida, who was hoping to confuse the champ with his defense-first strategy, did tag Weidman with some strong strikes in the final two rounds — wobbling the American — but he hung on, taking Machida down in the final round to help secure his unanimous victory. UFC 175 proved Weidman could take a fight the distance, and with two title defenses, the man who knocked off The Spider can no longer be considered underrated or on the rise. He's arrived — and should be a mainstay in the middleweight division for years to come.

TALE OF THE TAPE

BORN

UNITED STATES

D.O.B.
1984/06/17

HEIGHT
6'0"

WEIGHT
185 lb.

ASSOCIATION
Serra-Longo
Fight Team

NICKNAME
All-American

Above: Ronda Rousey slugs Miesha Tate as she defends her UFC women's bantamweight title at UFC 168. Right: Rousey connects with the head of Sara McMann at UFC 170. Rousey won the match via a TKO on strikes, her first victory not via submission.

IN A SENSE, she's come out of nowhere. But for Ronda Rousey, she's been here all along. Now that she's on the big stage, Rousey — the UFC women's undefeated bantamweight champion — isn't leaving anytime soon. The most dominant women's mixed martial artist the world has ever seen, Rousey is nearly undefeatable, showing no signs of stopping or slowing down. If the streak continues, she may forever be in a league of her own.

Born in California and raised in North Dakota, Rousey grew up the daughter of a famed judoka champion, her mother

AnnMaria. By 17, Rousey herself would qualify for the 2008 Summer Olympics in judo, winning bronze, the first American woman to claim the honor. Two years later, after working two bartending jobs and struggling to make ends meet, the woman nicknamed "Rowdy" entered her first MMA bout.

She drew inspiration from her father, who took his own life when Rousey was just eight years old after battling a debilitating back injury. Her dad always called her a "sleeper" — Rousey was born with the umbilical cord wrapped around her neck and had trouble speaking at an early age. Not only did this "sleeper" become an Olympic medalist and UFC champion, she's outspoken and unafraid to speak her mind. Her verbal spats with opponents, both in person and via Twitter, are famous, particularly her long war of words with archrival Miesha Tate. But Rousey isn't all talk — she backed those words up, dislocating Tate's elbow when she refused to tap out in their Strikeforce bout in 2012.

Sporting a 10-0 lifetime record in the ring, the women's number one pound-for-pound fighter in the world hasn't just been unstoppable — she's been untouchable. Rousey's first six octagon wins came via armbar, her signature move. Nine of those ten victories? All in the first round. But it's not simply her dominance on the ground. Rousey's judo, notably the ability to hip toss opponents at will, is what sets up those nasty armbars. "I believed that from my judo alone I could win every fight," she told ESPN. Once on the mat, she is predatory, hunting for the finish. "I've been training fighters for 15 years and I've never seen anything like Ronda Rousey," said her coach Edmond Tarverdyan.

It took UFC president Dana White, however, some convincing to include women in the UFC. "I don't know how the women's thing is going to go," he said before Rousey's bout with Liz Carmouche in early 2013 at UFC 157 — the first all-female bout in the UFC — which Rousey won at 4:49 of the first round by, what else, armbar. Promotions like Strikeforce and Invicta had carried women's fights before, but the UFC balked at a female division for years, citing lack of depth to carry competitive matches. Rousey's captivating personality and ability to put on a show changed that thinking, and the UFC signed her as the first female fighter in November 2012. The organization finally had its first marketable female star.

Rousey's fame has extended beyond the ring as well, including guest spots on the late-night TV circuit, a cover shot on *ESPN* magazine's "The Body Issue" and a burgeoning acting career that has seen her land a role in Entourage. This follows in the footsteps of

another women's MMA pioneer, Gina Curano, who left the sport to pursue Hollywood. With Rousey dominating the bantamweight division, talk of the two bombshells one day meeting in the ring increases daily.

In the meantime, Rousey keeps winning. Tate is the only opponent who's made it out of the first round against Rousey, nearly going the distance at UFC 168 after their spell as coaches on *The Ultimate Fighter*. The two mortal enemies verbally sparred with each other for the entire season of the show, and in the ring, Rousey put an exclamation mark on their war of words by cranking Tate's arm for the win at 58 seconds of the third round.

After the victory, Rousey delivered a devastating liver shot to former Olympic wrestler Sara McMann at UFC 170 only 56 days after disposing of Tate, the fastest title defense in UFC history. The victory proved Rousey could headline a card on her own. Her next win proved her TKO finish of McMann wasn't a fluke, as she knocked out Alexis Davis in 16 seconds at UFC 175 — tied for the UFC's second fastest KO.

Rousey is many things: an Olympic judo bronze medalist, a UFC champion, an armbar specialist, a sex symbol and a money maker. And the best part? She's just getting started.

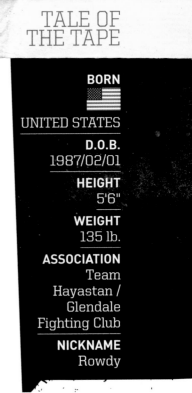

TALE OF
THE TAPE

BORN

UNITED STATES

D.O.B.
1987/02/01

HEIGHT
5'6"

WEIGHT
135 lb.

ASSOCIATION
Team
Hayastan /
Glendale
Fighting Club

NICKNAME
Rowdy

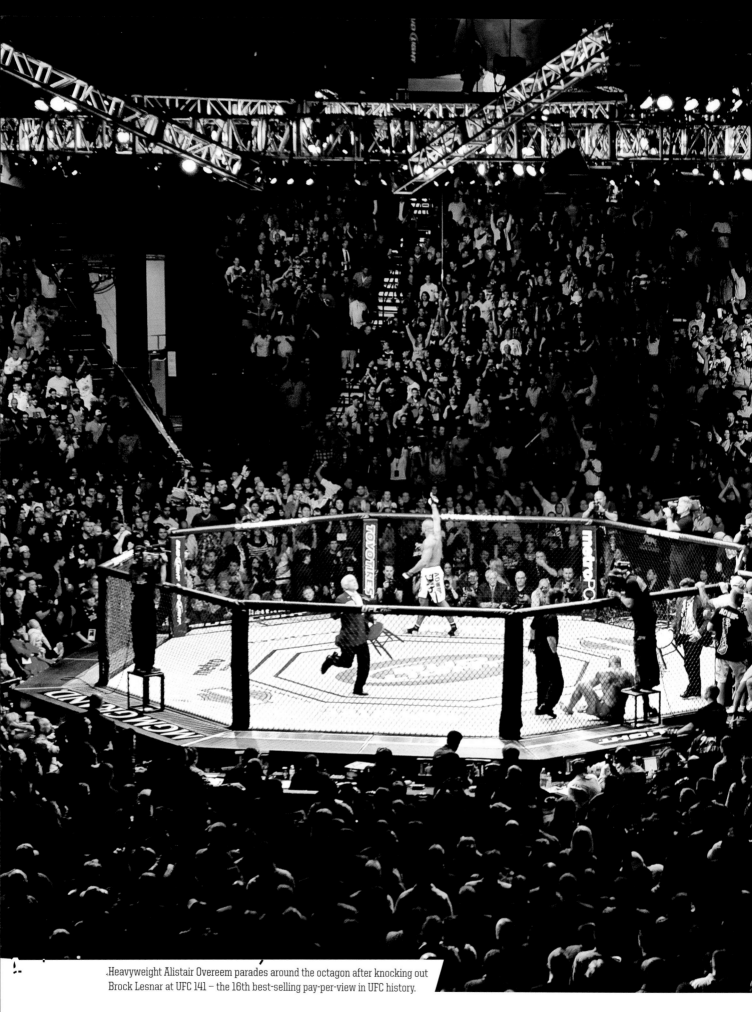

.Heavyweight Alistair Overeem parades around the octagon after knocking out
Brock Lesnar at UFC 141 – the 16th best-selling pay-per-view in UFC history.

WINNING FIGHTS AND MAKING MONEY

MAKING MONEY IS the biggest reason a promoter promotes a fight. Mixed martial arts matchmaking is all about reading the public and trying to figure who fans will pay to watch go toe to toe. If it's done correctly, says UFC president Dana White, then everyone will be happy. "If you put two guys in the octagon and have them fight, that [can cross] language barriers, ethnic barriers, everything. In the United States, they all want to see Americans beat Canadians or the English . . . the UFC is a very international brand."

Above: Donald "Cowboy" Cerrone knocks out Melvin Guillard at UFC 150. The fighters earned Fight of the Night bonuses for their slugfest. Right: A downtrodden Matt Hughes reflects on his loss to BJ Penn at UFC 123.

As a major professional sport, mixed martial arts promotions, like the UFC, operate differently from other top-grossing North American sports like football and baseball in that performance is only one of the criteria used when deciding if a competitor will vie for a title or, more important, be part of a main event. In all the major professional sports — whether they are team or individual — playoffs or tournaments are used to decide who gets a chance to compete for the championship. Fight promoters, however, do not choose who fights for belts at main events based solely on win-loss records. Sometimes a fighter that a promoter believes will sell the most tickets or pay-per-view buys will get the nod.

It's a phenomenon that would never be accepted in baseball or hockey. Imagine if those in charge of Major League Baseball decided that, as long as they had winning records, the New York Yankees and Los Angeles Dodgers would appear in the World Series every year because they are the two largest TV markets in the United States. It would never fly. Yet, this sort of matchmaking happens all the time in mixed martial arts.

At the UFC it's up to White, matchmaker Joe Silva and the rest of the staff to figure out which fighters they need to promote and how the promotion should be done. Sounds easy, but knowing which fighters are worthy of main-event status is actually a little more complicated than it looks.

WIN AND YOU'RE IN

At the end of the day, winning does matter. Being better than your opponent more often than not is always high on the list of criteria for matchmakers, and good fighters who win a lot will eventually earn a title shot and usually a position in a main event. Fight fans want to see the best

win, you learn," said Renzo Gracie. "You win the fight or you learn."

Many of the greatest fighters in UFC history became legends only after they lost and returned to competition as better competitors. Multiple-time champions like Georges St-Pierre, Matt Hughes and Randy Couture were known for the way they used defeats as learning experiences and motivation for future fights. "If you haven't lost in this sport yet," Hughes famously said, "then you haven't fought the right guys."

WINNING ISN'T THE ONLY THING: PART TWO

UFC president Dana White has made it clear that he is more concerned with fighters entertaining the audience than winning all the time. This can be illustrated by welterweight Jon Fitch's career. At the time he was released by the UFC in 2013 he had a record with the promotion of 14-3-1, with one of his losses coming to welterweight champion Georges St-Pierre and another to eventual champ Johny Hendricks. Even though he was a consistent winner, the majority of Fitch's wins were by decision and saw him use his considerable wrestling skills to control the fight. The UFC encourages its fighters to take chances by offering performance bonuses at all its events, including Performance of the Night and Fight of the Night. When Fitch was released, Dana White said it was because he'd won only one of his last four fights. And while that may have been the determining factor for his pink slip, the reality was that Fitch was a fighter the majority of fans thought boring — and that is the kiss of death.

On the opposite end of the spectrum is Melvin Guillard. The Louisiana native who signed with the promotion in 2005 and lost three of his first six matches lasted for 10 years and 23 bouts before he was canned in 2014. Guillard ended up winning only 13 of those 23 bouts, but the reason he was allowed to stay for so long was his penchant for taking risks to get the knockout, which, more often than not, got him in trouble. As the big swinger said before fighting Donald Cerrone at UFC 150, "I don't even want it to be a technical fight. I want to turn it into an all-out brawl. I know right now that's probably what the fans want to see and we can make it the Fight of the Night because we can go in there and brawl it out." Guillard caught Cerrone early, but Cerrone was able to weather the storm and come back to knock Guillard out — all in the first round! The scrap lived up to Guillard's prefight hype, and each fighter took home $60,000 for Fight of the Night.

versus the best — or at the very least a fight that either combatant is capable of winning. So even if a fighter has all the other qualities that make him a box office draw, if he can't win, he can't fight for a title.

WINNING ISN'T THE ONLY THING

Although winning is important, winning all the time is not a necessity for a successful and popular fighter. Unlike boxing, where main-event fighters often have long unbeaten records, it is the rare case that an MMA star hasn't taken at least a couple of losses. Aside from the parity in the MMA world right now, the reason largely has a lot to do with the nature of fighting. There are so many more ways to win or lose a fight in MMA that even the best fighters in the world can be caught by surprise. So losing is not the end of a career for an MMA fighter. In fact, a good loss can be a good thing. It keeps fighters hungry and fans on the edge of their seats. Most of the great fighters look at losing in a positive light. "Even if you don't

GOLD (AROUND THE WAIST) IS MONEY

When you look at the list of all-time highest-grossing pay-per-views in UFC history, it's clearly important that something other than bragging rights be at stake. The gold around a champion's waist is the ultimate enticement. Of the top 20 highest-selling UFC pay-per-views of all-time, only one doesn't feature a main event with a UFC title at stake. That event was UFC 141, which was headlined by a heavyweight bout between Brock Lesnar and Alistair Overeem. Title fights involving Lesnar also happen to own the top two spots on the list, proving that the heavyweight's drawing power was simply immense.

BIGGER IS BETTER

In the world of mixed martial arts matchmaking, bigger is usually better. The majority of the best-selling UFC pay-per-views were headlined by heavyweights or light heavyweights. Over the last decade, welterweight Georges St-Pierre and middleweight Anderson Silva have been the two most dominating and famous fighters in the UFC, yet neither of them made as much on a per-fight basis as heavyweight Brock Lesnar.

The reasons behind this have a lot to do with why people are compelled to watch a professional fight. Ultimately, fight fans want to be able to identify the toughest

SIZE MATTERS

Size rules when it comes to the three biggest purse earners in the UFC and their per-fight pay-out.

1 BROCK LESNAR
HEIGHT
6'3"
WEIGHT
266 lb.
WEIGHT CLASS
Heavyweight
TOTAL UFC BOUTS
7
CAREER UFC PURSE*
$2,825,000.00
PER-FIGHT UFC PURSE AVERAGE
$403,571.00

2 ANDERSON SILVA
HEIGHT
6'2"
WEIGHT
185 lb.
WEIGHT CLASS
Middleweight
TOTAL UFC BOUTS
18
CAREER UFC PURSE*
$4,297,000.00
PER-FIGHT UFC PURSE AVERAGE
$238,722.00

3 GEORGES ST-PIERRE
HEIGHT
5'11"
WEIGHT
170 lb.
WEIGHT CLASS
Welterweight
TOTAL UFC BOUTS
21
CAREER UFC PURSE*
$4,452,000.00
PER-FIGHT UFC PURSE AVERAGE
$212,000.00

* Purse amounts are estimates. Fight of the Night and Performance of the Night bonuses are included. Sponsorship and pay-per-view shares are not included.

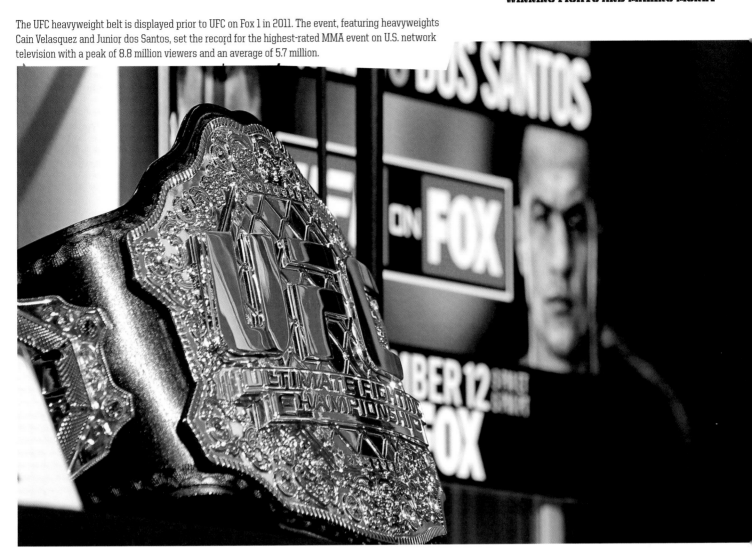

The UFC heavyweight belt is displayed prior to UFC on Fox 1 in 2011. The event, featuring heavyweights Cain Velasquez and Junior dos Santos, set the record for the highest-rated MMA event on U.S. network television with a peak of 8.8 million viewers and an average of 5.7 million.

guy on the planet, and since a good big man will almost always beat a good little man of equal skill, whoever holds the heavyweight title should theoretically be able to beat any of the other champions at the lower weight divisions. This is what makes heavyweight title fights so compelling. The heavyweight champion is the king of the jungle.

During times when there hasn't been a strong heavyweight champion, the light heavyweights will often take center stage. Chuck Liddell, Tito Ortiz and Randy Couture were all light heavyweight champions who were able to draw huge dollars from big fights. Of course, it helped Couture that he also fought as a heavyweight.

CHARACTER AND STORY

A compelling mixed martial arts bout draws on the same need for dynamic characters and great stories as a Hollywood film. Fighters with big personalities sell more tickets and pay-per-views, so they tend to get far more opportunities than those fighters with equal skills and

records who can't flash a multi-watt smile or get by on their bravado.

Chael Sonnen is a perfect example of a fighter who can lose in bunches and use his personality to stay relevant. The abrasive and arrogant scrapper's most infamous moment came after he defeated Brian Stann at UFC 136 in October 2011. Instead of talking about his win over Stann, Sonnen grabbed the mic and issued the following challenge to UFC middleweight champion Anderson Silva, who was sitting cageside:

"Anderson Silva you absolutely suck. Super Bowl weekend the biggest rematch in the business. I'm calling you out and we're upping the stakes. I beat you — you leave the division. You beat me, I leave the UFC forever."

The crowd went crazy, and Sonnen's play took the MMA world by surprise. Most fighters were respectful after a fight, usually complimenting a defeated opponent, or at most paying their respects to the current champion while asking UFC president Dana White for an opportunity to fight for a title. With his challenge, Sonnen had pretty much guaranteed he'd be getting a future title shot at the champion. It didn't really matter that Silva had beaten Sonnen already — albeit in very close match — or that other legitimate contenders may have deserved a title shot first. Sonnen had generated interest in a future bout with Silva that would lead to ticket and pay-per-view sales and plenty of dollars in the pockets of the UFC, Sonnen and even Silva.

Sonnen's promise may have been shocking, but it was hardly a piece of original work. Known as the "Loser Leaves Town" promo, Sonnen's play was one that had been used in professional wrestling for years and was especially popular in the time when professional wrestling promotions were regionalized. Typically, two wrestlers would embark on a series of weekly matches, with the "stakes" growing each subsequent week. Once the promoter felt the "feud" had run its course, one of the wrestlers would issue a "Loser Leaves Town" challenge. Interest would

usually be high, and after the final bout the loser would indeed leave town and move on to another territory. Of course, once enough time passed, he'd often come back and hope enough of the locals had forgotten his previous promise to not return.

In Sonnen's case, his skill on the microphone did pay off. He was eventually rewarded with a rematch with Anderson Silva nine months later at UFC 148. Before the event, Sonnen used his time in front of reporters to generate even more interest in the fight. "Anderson Silva is as fake as Mike Tyson was. They called him the hardest, 'the baddest man in the world,' but he wasn't even the toughest guy in America and we had to sit through and listen to that over and over again as he fought lots of tomato cans."

UFC 148 attracted over a million pay-per-view buys and ranks in the top 10 of the most popular UFC pay-per-views of all time. Some of the credit for the success of this event must go to Sonnen and some to a wrestler from the '70s by the name of "Superstar" Billy Graham, whose original speech Sonnen copied almost word for word when he issued his challenge to Silva.

Below: Chael Sonnen trash-talks at the weigh-in for his light heavyweight title fight with Jon Jones at UFC 159. Jones defeated Sonnen soundly. Right: Sonnen gets no respect from middleweight champion Anderson Silva at the weigh-in prior to UFC 117. Anderson defended his title against Sonnen.

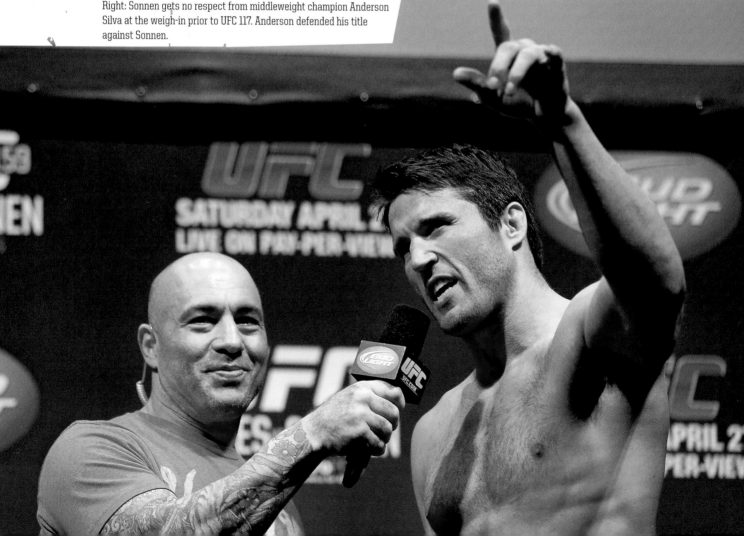

Another fighter who used professional wrestling tactics effectively was Brock Lesnar, arguably the most marketable UFC star in history. Lesnar has appeared in the main event of five of the top 20 most popular UFC pay-per-views of all time — four of which are in the top 10, including the top two! It's a stunning achievement for someone who fought a total of eight mixed martial arts bouts.

Lesnar, however, wasn't your garden-variety heavyweight. More than any other fighter in UFC history, he possessed the qualities that mixed martial arts fans found irresistible. He usually weighed in at 266 and looked like a bodybuilder. Despite this bulk he was also agile and shockingly quick for a man his size, and his athleticism allowed him to become one of the premier amateur wrestlers in the world. Later, as a professional wrestler, Lesnar performed maneuvers normally done by men literally half his size.

Lesnar also knew how to "cut a promo," or hype an upcoming match, by simply talking on the microphone — skills he learned during his time as a top star on the World Wrestling Entertainment circuit. After defeating Heath Herring at UFC 87, his third MMA fight, he jumped up on the cage and yelled, "Can you see me now!" It was one line, but it electrified the crowd. Throughout his career he did as much to build his reputation with his voice as with his fists. In an early promotional video Lesnar introduces himself by saying, "I am Brock Lesnar. I am an ass kicker." His most notorious promo happened at the end of UFC 100. After thoroughly dominating Frank Mir in a redemption match, Lesnar, instead of shaking hands and being gracious, told the crowd, "Frank Mir has horse shoes up his ass! I told him that a year ago. Tonight I pulled it out of his ass and beat him with it!" With the crowd booing him he continued. "I'm going to go home tonight. I'm going to have a Coors Light — not a Bud Light because Bud Light won't pay me.

I'll hang out with my friends and family. Hell, I might even get on top of my wife tonight." Lesnar's speech was pure heel, and it absolutely dumbfounded the audience. In other words, it was perfect. He apologized later for his remarks, however, but in the long run Lesnar's trash talk only enhanced his marketability to UFC fans.

It's very difficult to get an accurate total of career earnings for UFC fighters. The majority of their fight-related income comes from the purse they get — usually more for a win than a loss. The rest comes from their cut of the total pay-per-view revenue (which only ever goes to the premier fighters on a card). Georges St-Pierre is considered to be the top earner in UFC history, while Brock Lesnar is in third place. The fact that Lesnar earned his money in about a third of the number of fights as St-Pierre is an indication of just how popular Lesnar was with the buying public. He, of all the UFC fighters in history, was the one who had the most success getting consumers to spend money on UFC events.

And let's not forget that the men and women who fight in the UFC, or any other big-market MMA promotion, are building brands at the same time as they are building their fighting image. Stars like St-Pierre and Jon Jones have locked down big endorsements with mainstream sports companies and other non-sport-related businesses, worth big dollars. For elite fighters with marketing potential, the best money may come from outside the ring.

ALL THIS TO say that mixed martial arts is, above all else, a business. When it comes to matchmaking, the potential to make money is a more important consideration to the promoters than setting up a fight between the two best fighters. Sometimes promoters get lucky and the best money-making match will end up featuring the two best combatants — and that is a real win for all involved.

On the grandest stages, MMA will always be about creating the most intriguing, but not necessarily the best, matchups for the pay-per-view buying public. It is the only major sport where the customer really does come first. "We know what fights people want to see," said UFC president Dana White. "We have different types of fights, ones that hardcore MMA fans are into, and then fights that break through, that spill over into mainstream that people will pay per view to see. I know what fights people want because I'm the biggest fight fan there is."

Brock Lesnar mugs for the fans after his second-round submission of Shane Carwin to win the UFC heavyweight title at UFC 116. The bout is the second-best-selling UFC pay-per-view of all time.

MONEY MAKERS

Above: Tito Ortiz employs some ground and pound offense in 2006 to defeat Ken Shamrock for the third time in as many fights. Right: Ortiz lands a solid blow to Rashad Evans at UFC 73, which was scored a unanimous draw.

TITO ORTIZ WASN'T always the most professional or polished fighter, but in the era following early UFC stars Royce Gracie and Ken Shamrock, "the Huntington Beach Bad Boy" was a polarizing figure who earned a loyal following for his heel act and swagger, establishing him as one of the biggest draws in MMA.

And that swagger set the stage for one of the most important events in UFC history. UFC 40: Vendetta took place on November 22, 2002. The marquee bout featured Ortiz and Shamrock. The seeds were sown three

years earlier when Ortiz faced Guy Mezger at UFC 19 in 1999. And even that fight had vendetta-like circumstances. Mezger — part of Ken Shamrock's Lion's Den team — had defeated Ortiz in 1997 at UFC 13. Then a relative unknown, Ortiz found a spot on the card through the work of his college wrestling coach and UFC fighter Paul Herrera. At the tournament, Ortiz, a two-time National Junior College Athletic Association champion with Golden West College, acquitted himself well and found himself fighting in the final round against Mezger. The greenhorn pressed

his advantage early, but Mezger caught him with a guillotine choke and submitted him.

Over the next two years Ortiz fought twice, winning both times. His reward? The main-event rematch with Mezger at UFC 19. Ortiz overpowered Mezger, but his postfight antics are what fans remember most. Ortiz put on a custom T-shirt with a slogan that belittled Mezger with sexist and homophobic slurs. Shamrock, in Mezger's corner, was enraged by the lack of respect and tried to fight Ortiz right then and there. A war of words ensued and a rivalry was created — just like that. But their meeting at UFC 40: Vendetta would have to wait, as shortly thereafter, Shamrock abandoned the UFC to pursue a wrestling career with the WWF.

In the interim, Ortiz was booked to fight Ken's stepbrother, Frank Shamrock. Despite possessing a noticeable size advantage, Ortiz was beaten by Shamrock in the fourth round when he simply ran out of gas. Afterward Frank invited Ortiz to train with him. "I taught him about vascular conditioning and mindset," said Shamrock. The experience was invaluable to Ortiz, who defeated Wanderlei Silva in his next fight for the light heavyweight belt. He reeled off four straight title defenses over the next two years.

By the time UFC 40 arrived, a lot had changed for Ortiz, the UFC and Ken Shamrock. Ortiz, now with a belt, bleached blond hair and a cocky attitude, was one of the stars of the promotion now owned by Zuffa, the company headed by Dana White and Lorenzo and Frank Fertitta. Ken Shamrock's turn with the WWF had made him mixed martial arts' most recognizable athlete, and he and Ortiz were on a collision course.

Zuffa had staged seven money-losing pay-per-views since taking over the UFC, but with Ortiz as the heel and Shamrock returning to the promotion for the first time since 1996, hopes were high. The fight generated over $1.5 million in gate revenue, at the time a new record for the UFC, and the pay-per-view numbers were even more impressive with 150,000 buys for the event

— more than double any of the previous Zuffa events.

With the win, Ortiz's drawing power — especially when pitted against another top-flight fighter — became wildly evident. By 2005, as Zuffa began to find its market, almost every UFC PPV event sold more than six figures. Still, it was Ortiz who proved to be the promotion's biggest draw. UFC 59, featuring Ortiz vs. Forrest Griffin, established a new company record by exceeding 400,000 buys, and later that same year, his rematch with Ken Shamrock at UFC 61 (which Ortiz won) garnered an incredible 775,000 buys.

The final and most powerful proof of Ortiz's drawing power was his second fight against Chuck Liddell at UFC 66, which attracted over one million buys. Despite being the financial apex of Ortiz's career, it marked the beginning of his slide into mediocrity as a fighter. After losing to Liddell for the second time, Ortiz won only one of his next eight fights over a six-year period before retiring in 2012.

Despite his eroding skill, Ortiz's box office appeal remains shockingly strong. At 39, he came out of retirement to sign with Bellator for one more kick at the can, submitting Alexander Shlemenko in the first round at Bellator 120 in May 2014. The win secured his first victory in nearly three years, and with the confidence boost, his fans are almost assured another heel turn to cap his wildly successful career.

TALE OF THE TAPE

BORN
🇺🇸
UNITED STATES

D.O.B.
1975/01/23

HEIGHT
6'2"

WEIGHT
205 lb.

ASSOCIATION
Team Punishment

NICKNAME
The Huntington Beach Bad Boy

CHAEL SONNEN

Above: Chael Sonnen works to end the reign of middleweight champ Anderson Silva at UFC 117 in 2010. Sonnen fought well before succumbing to an armbar late in the fifth round. Right: Sonnen defeats Michael Bisping at UFC on Fox 2.

CHAEL SONNEN IS a piece of work: he'd probably be the first to admit it. But he's also a dangerous fighter who has challenged for belts in several different weight classes. Along the way, "the People's Champ" has endeared himself to fans as the greatest trash talker in the UFC. In the process, he became one of the highest-paid athletes in mixed martial arts.

As enigmatic as they come, the 37-year-old took a page out of professional wrestling and crafted his persona, "the American Gangster," as a fast-talking, larger-than-life character.

But Sonnen's legit. He's a businessman who co-owns a pizza parlor, has dabbled in local politics and even holds a real estate license. He also authored the book *The Voice of Reason: A VIP Pass to Enlightenment*, in which he discusses and disputes his failed test for testosterone replacement therapy (TRT) and a money laundering conviction. So even when he's not stepping into the octagon, he's got money and his reputation on his mind.

It wasn't always this way. Sonnen's early career was rather inglorious, and it took the lightweight more than 20 professional fights to crack the UFC roster. Born in Milwaukie, Oregon, and raised in West Linn, a suburb of Portland, the high school wrestling star didn't last long in his first UFC stint, sporting a 1-2 record before being released in 2006. But Sonnen's tenacity, honed trying to impress a strict father and later refocused while wrestling at the University of Oregon, helped the big-shouldered, 6-foot-1 fighter with the 74-inch reach climb his way back up the MMA ladder, returning full time to the UFC in 2009 as a middleweight.

In a sport now populated by myriad personalities, the Oregon native stands out. He lists Pope John Paul II as his hero on his official UFC bio. He's maintained a long-standing feud not only with Wanderlei Silva but all of Brazil as well, culminating in the two fighters nearly brawling outside the octagon as coaches on *The Ultimate Fighter Brazil 3* in 2014.

But in the ring, Sonnen backs up his talking. The wrestler has averaged nearly four takedowns per fight and a 66 percent takedown defense during his UFC career. Since 2009, his time fighting at middleweight has been well spent. He won three of his first four fights, reeling off victories over big names like Dan Miller, Yushin Okami and Nate Marquardt. The wins, and his mouth, nabbed him a title fight with none other than perennial champion Anderson Silva. No one, except for maybe Sonnen himself, thought he had much of a shot at UFC 117. However, the bout was named 2010 Fight of the Year by mmafighting.com, with the People's Champ giving the champion one of his stiffest tests to date, grounding, pounding and outwrestling the Brazilian. Sonnen even led on the judges' scorecards. But Silva's spirited comeback in the fifth and final round, capped off by a triangle choke, sealed any talk of upset.

After the fight, Sonnen tested positive for excessive levels of TRT and was banished for the year. The middleweight took the loss and suspension in stride, resurfacing with big wins against American middleweight Brian Stann and British brawler Michael

Bisping — both within a three-month span.

The wins gave Sonnen reason to run his mouth again. His wish? A rematch with Silva. Once again, the wrestler dominated early, but a misfired spinning elbow in the second round opened a window for Silva, and Sonnen's night ended on the ground in a flurry of head punches. UFC president Dana White told the *Jim Rome Show* the following week that Sonnen shared something no one had expected to hear: that he had "so much respect" for Silva. Sonnen said to White that he felt the Brazilian break in the first round of UFC 148 when he was dominating, and that Silva's comeback in the second was a remarkable feat he'd never seen in all his years of fighting. UFC 148 sold one million PPV buys and ranks in the top 10 all-time most successful matches in UFC history, largely because of Sonnen's trash talk. The respect he dished out, albeit privately, was certainly a rarity.

When the chance came to take on light heavyweight Jon Jones in 2013 for a title shot on less than two weeks' notice, Sonnen jumped. He lost, handily, but proved himself a company man — if not always up for a quick buck.

The People's Champ knows that no matter what, there will always be an audience for those willing to speak their minds. But, with a surprise retirement in June 2014 after more doping allegations, Sonnen will likely be doing his talking from the broadcast booth — at least for a while.

TALE OF THE TAPE

BORN

🇺🇸

UNITED STATES

D.O.B.
1977/04/03

HEIGHT
6'1"

WEIGHT
205 lb.

ASSOCIATION
Team Quest

NICKNAME
The People's Champ

FORREST GRIFFIN

Above: Forrest Griffin slugs Stephan Bonnar in his victory at UFC 62, a reprise of their match at *The Ultimate Fighter* series 1 finale, which Griffin also won. Right: Griffin kicks Tito Ortiz at UFC 148. The win over Ortiz marked Griffin's last professional bout.

FOR AN ATHLETE to truly be considered among the best in his profession, many things must conspire for him. Being in the right place at the right time is often one of those things, and that is exactly what happened to Forrest Griffin. As the first winner of *The Ultimate Fighter* TV series, he was a centerpiece in the most important fight in UFC history.

Griffin didn't set out to become a mixed martial artist. Growing up in Augusta, Georgia, the rambunctious, goofy kid wore No. 67 and played defensive tackle on his high school football team. Using his 6-foot-3 frame, he terrorized opposing quarterbacks.

But before he even set foot in the ring, Griffin embarked on a career in law enforcement, working in the sheriff's office in Augusta. Stepping into a local MMA gym to help hone skills he figured he'd need as a police officer changed Griffin's outlook. His first bout came against UFC Hall of Famer Dan Severn, who fought way back at UFC 4 against men like Ken Shamrock, Tank Abbott and Royce Gracie. The Georgia rookie lost to the veteran, but he must have learned something because

Griffin put up eight straight victories over a two-year period, finally catching the eye of the UFC in 2005.

UFC president Dana White convinced the exuberant Griffin to compete on the debut season of a reality television show about 16 fighters competing for a contract with the organization. The finale, broadcast on Spike TV, would be one of the first times the UFC was seen on a non-pay-per-view channel. If the program failed to draw numbers or deliver in entertainment value, the promotion risked staying on the fringes of the sports landscape, and they were desperately in need of cash flow.

When Griffin and Stephan Bonnar stepped into the octagon that night to face each other, everything changed. Back and forth they went, pummeling each other for three rounds. When one fighter blinked, the other climbed back into contention. Griffin was scored the winner, and Bonnar fell to his knees, gutted. But because of the heart Bonnar showed, White offered him a contract as well. The slugfest convinced casual fans and sponsors that MMA had a future, and White and the Fertitta brothers, owners of Zuffa Entertainment, never looked back.

Griffin won his next two bouts before meeting bad boy Tito Ortiz in 2006, a split-decision victory that fostered a strong rivalry. Griffin then pulled off an improbable submission win at UFC 76 in 2007 against Mauricio "Shogun" Rua, who at the time was a number one contender for the light heavyweight crown. But Griffin busted up his shoulder during the fight and needed a year off to heal. Good thing he did — when he showed up as an underdog against Quinton "Rampage" Jackson, not many believed he could unseat the champ. Despite taking some early first-round damage, including a nasty uppercut, Griffin survived, and they battled four more rounds to one of the best MMA fights that year.

The reign was short-lived as Griffin lost the belt in his first defense to Rashad Evans later that year. He was further embarrassed by Anderson Silva in 2009 during a nontitle fight at UFC 101 when the longtime middleweight belt holder made Griffin look like a tomato can, knocking him out. Griffin rebounded with another win versus Ortiz and division stalwart Rich Franklin, but he took a one-sided loss to Rua in their rematch.

His final fight with Ortiz was rather inglorious, if only for Griffin's antics following the three-round match. Despite winning the bout, Griffin bolted from the ring before the decision was announced, prompting White to chase after Griffin, who subsequently returned only to snatch the microphone from ring interviewer Joe Rogan's hand so he could interview Ortiz himself. Ortiz had been planning a retirement speech, and White was livid. "I love Forrest Griffin," he said at the postfight press conference. "But he gets a little kooky sometimes." Turns out it would be Griffin's final appearance as well. The recurring shoulder injury that plagued him throughout his career and a more recently torn ACL forced him into retirement.

Griffin left MMA with a 19-7 record, but most will remember him for one fight: a war against Bonnar, fought under the spotlight of reality television, that showcased the two warriors doing battle for three rounds. This past year, they stood side by side as recent entrants into the UFC Hall of Fame, their names uttered in the same breath once again.

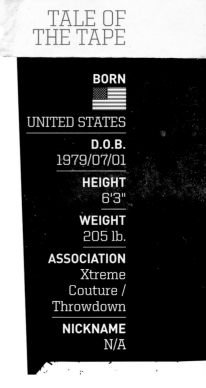

TALE OF THE TAPE

BORN

UNITED STATES

D.O.B.
1979/07/01

HEIGHT
6'3"

WEIGHT
205 lb.

ASSOCIATION
Xtreme Couture / Throwdown

NICKNAME
N/A

NICK DIAZ

Above: Nick Diaz punches Georges St-Pierre at UFC 158 in 2013. Right: Diaz strikes BJ Penn at UFC 137 in 2011. His win over Penn was his 11th straight victory.

HE'S GOT A fighter's face. A mean, mugging face that stares out from across the octagon at his opponents. A face that looks as if he was born to do this. A face you don't forget. Maybe that's why, in the span of the last decade, Nick Diaz has gone from scrawny kid to one of the biggest draws in MMA today.

Nickolas Robert Diaz grew up rough in Stockton, a city south of Sacramento in the San Joaquin Valley. The oldest of two brothers — younger sibling Nate scraps at lightweight — the high school dropout was bullied as a teen but found reprieve in karate

lessons and watching early UFC fights. By 18, the 6-foot-1, 170-pound welterweight had already defeated his first opponent by triangle choke. Now 30, he's fought 35 more times since that late summer day in 2001. Name the organization and the mercurial Diaz has donned the gloves: UFC. Pride. Elite XC. Strikeforce. Dream. And he's stepped into the ring in far-flung locales like Japan, Hawaii and Montreal.

Throughout his career, Diaz has appeared cryptic and prone to controversy. He has twice been disciplined for violating drug

policies. At Pride 33, remembered first for his rare gogoplata submission, Diaz even had the win overturned for having had marijuana levels 11 times the legal limit. He was also suspended one year following his interim welterweight championship fight with Carlos Condit at UFC 143 in 2012 after a positive test for marijuana metabolites.

There's little doubt Diaz is as talented as they come. Well rounded and unpredictable in style, with submission skills that rival most welterweights, his recent fights have rarely gone to the ground because of opponents' respect for his ground game.

Diaz was a jiu-jitsu prodigy, so early in his career he added deceptive boxing skills to his arsenal, making his standup equal to the task versus established strikers. Take the Robbie Lawler fight in 2004 at UFC 47. The Vegas bout featured two young prospects, with Lawler slightly older and the heavier puncher. Diaz was up to his usual antics — trash-talking, dropping his hands, egging Lawler on — and it was working. When Diaz popped Lawler a few times in the first round, Lawler's anger got the best of him and he charged Diaz like a raging bull. The energy in the Mandalay Bay surged. In the second, after Lawler connected hard to Diaz's face, the Stockton native returned the favor and stung Lawler with a short, over-the-top right hook. Fight over. Decision by knockout. Even announcer Joe Rogan was in disbelief at the outcome. It was an early indicator: expect the unexpected with Diaz.

Whether Diaz intended to become a heel or a villain is up for debate. But at some point he embraced the role. If it sold tickets, so be it. He's bristly during interviews. He swears like a trucker. He flips the bird at other fighters. In his final defense of the Strikeforce welterweight title, Diaz said to well-respected journalist Ariel Helwani: "I feel like you instigate fights. I mean that's your job, but where I come from, people like that get slapped." In 2006, the Stockton product even ended up in an altercation in the hospital with Joe Riggs after their three-round scrap at UFC 57.

Diaz owns a clothing line with the slogan "Don't Be Scared, Homie," a now-infamous line he uttered to K.J. Noons at an Elite XC event in Honolulu in 2008. And when he finally got a title shot versus Georges St-Pierre at UFC 158, Diaz immortalized the phrase "wolf tickets," claiming UFC president Dana White and St-Pierre were bluffing the public, making Diaz into someone he isn't just to hype the fight. The bout sold 1.1 million buys, tied for third most in UFC history. And then Diaz inexplicably quit.

The guy from "the 209" is as true as they come. He's fiercely loyal to those around him, especially younger brother Nate, whom Nick corners whenever the lightweight steps into the ring. And, as unexpected as his opponents have found him, his fans shouldn't count Diaz out yet, either. The man who also competes in triathlons and has even once boxed professionally has started his own hometown promotion in 2013, WAR MMA. He's hinted at returning to the UFC, but for a price — $3 to $5 per pay-per-view buy — which is typically reserved for the champions of the sport. If Diaz can prove he's worth it, we may not have seen the last of him.

TALE OF THE TAPE

BORN
UNITED STATES
D.O.B.
1983/08/02
HEIGHT
6'1"
WEIGHT
170 lb.
ASSOCIATION
Cesar Gracie Fight Team
NICKNAME
N/A

WANDERLEI SILVA

Above: Wanderlei Silva kicks Rich Franklin at their UFC 147 catchweight bout in 2012. Right: Silva knees Brian Stann in the head during their light heavyweight fight at UFC on FUEL TV 8. Silva scored a knockout for the win.

AT **49 FIGHTS** and still counting, it's a wonder that Wanderlei Silva is still standing, let alone fighting. "The Axe Murderer" has been one of the most feared mixed martial artists on the planet for the better part of the last two decades. And while the 37-year-old may be winding down his career, his legacy as one of the toughest men to ever enter the octagon will never abate.

Silva was born to scrap. His menacing look — a shaved, tattooed head; a 5-foot-11 body built like a Mac truck; and a no-holds-barred approach — has endeared him to fans. So too

does his technical ability in Muay Thai, wielding punches, knees and kicks in the clinch and destroying opponents with his formidable fists.

After a brief stint in the Brazilian military, Silva began bare-knuckle vale tudo fighting, a predecessor of MMA popular in the '90s that contained fewer rules and, consequently, more violence. His most famous early fight was in fact his first loss. Moving forward ferociously, Silva came at Artur Mariano with haymakers, but the fight was stopped briefly when Silva landed a legal head butt, opening up a severe cut on his own head. Instead of protecting himself, Silva continued using his head to punish Mariano. The doctor, however, stopped the bout when it was deemed Silva couldn't continue — that much blood was pouring from his face. It revealed just how fearless Silva truly was, and how far he was willing to go to prove his toughness.

There has never been any middle ground for Silva. It's either knock a man out or be knocked out. He knows no other way. In fact, the Brazilian hasn't won by submission since 1999. After establishing his no-holds-barred reputation in vale tudo, Silva debuted in the UFC in 1998. He lasted just 44 seconds in his first bout with the promotion, suffering a brutal KO at the hands of fellow countryman Vitor Belfort. Although he'd fight in the UFC several more times during this period, including a failed crack at Tito Ortiz's light heavyweight belt in 2000 at UFC 25, it was Silva's eventual move to Pride in Japan that established him as one of the premier MMA stars in the world.

Silva holds a laundry list of accomplishments in Pride: most wins, most knockouts and the longest win streak — 18 consecutive matches without a loss, including 13 knockouts.

Several men established themselves as worthy adversaries of the violent Brazilian. Japanese legend Kazushi Sakuraba fought Silva three times, never earning a win. Quinton "Rampage" Jackson suffered two of his most devastating losses at the hands of the Axe Murderer, including an over-the-ropes, face-first fall that goes down as one of the most devastating knockouts ever seen in Pride. That was at the height of Silva's power — he'd incur several losses as his Pride career wound down. By the time he fought Jackson a third and final time in the UFC, heavy knockout losses to Dan Henderson and Chuck Liddell had taken their toll. Rampage took advantage, stinging Silva with a strong left hook to the jaw that ended his night.

But Silva's electricity in the ring, win or lose, proved hard for the UFC to pass up, and since that night in 2008, he's fought six more

times, alternating between wins and losses, including a barn burner of a middleweight scrap against Brian Stann that ended in a Fight of the Night performance and a win for Silva. He's compiled a career significant strike accuracy of 40 percent in the UFC, landing 2.79 strikes per minute. As of 2014, his career MMA record stands at 35-12-1-1.

Perhaps a final bookend to his career, Silva coached *The Ultimate Fighter Brazil 3* in 2014 opposite Chael Sonnen, a noted rival whose dislike for Silva has long been boiling over. It culminated in a barroom-like shoving match outside the octagon caught on camera by the UFC. Although both men indicated they'd settle the score mano a mano after the near scrap, it will likely never happen. Both Sonnen and Silva were pulled from the scheduled fight due to issues related to performance enhancing drugs.

After a long, hard-fought career, Silva will go down as one of the more intimidating men to ever enter the ring, an old-school throwback who continued to endure throughout the years. He took punishment. He dished it out. And through it all, he has acted like a true warrior.

TALE OF THE TAPE

BORN

BRAZIL

D.O.B.
1976/07/03

HEIGHT
5'11"

WEIGHT
185 lb.

ASSOCIATION
Wand Fight Team

NICKNAME
The Axe Murderer

Above: Brock Lesnar celebrates after his second-round submission of Shane Carwin to win the UFC heavyweight title at UFC 116. Right: Lesnar trades punches with Heath Herring at UFC 87, a unanimous decision for Lesnar.

BROCK LESNAR HAS excelled in whatever sport he's chosen. The former college wrestling star has become a three-time WWE champion and UFC heavyweight titleholder. One thing is never in doubt with Lesnar: everything arrives larger than life. And so is the mark he left upon mixed martial arts.

Blessed with superhuman size, Lesnar, at 6 foot 3, tips the scales at 286 pounds, though he kept his fighting weight 20 pounds lighter during his brief UFC run. Born in a small town in North Dakota, he went undefeated as a high school wrestler, posting a 33-0 record

in his hometown of Webster. An All-American in the heavyweight class at the University of Minnesota, the massive Lesnar entered the world of professional wrestling, and in 2002, he became the youngest heavyweight champion in WWE's history when he defeated "the Rock." At just 25, it had taken him only two years to establish a name for himself. But he wasn't satisfied. Unafraid to take risks, Lesnar, wrestling's biggest star at the time, did a 180-degree turn and made a sojourn into the NFL in 2004 to try out for the Minnesota Vikings. He nearly made it, too, but the defensive tackle was a late cut and never played football again.

The North Dakota native then took on a new challenge: mixed martial arts. Under the tutelage of Greg Nelson, Lesnar fought Min-Soo Kim at Dynamite!! USA, ending the 2007 bout at just 1:09 to win his first foray into MMA. He used his well-honed promotional skills to begin calling out UFC heavyweights before he was even signed. He would soon get his chance.

Lesnar immediately became one of the faces of the UFC thanks to his name-brand recognition from pro wrestling. Seeking legitimacy and star power, the promotion embraced the move, and although Lesnar's crossover appeared gimmicky (especially after he suffered a quick exit at the hands of Frank Mir in his first bout), the multitalented athlete soon proved he could compete with the best in the world. He rebounded with wins over Heath Herring and UFC legend Randy Couture. And he wasn't finished.

A year and a half after Lesnar had lost his first UFC match, he was back to face Mir at UFC 100 for the heavyweight title. Lesnar rose to the occasion, in more ways than one. After defeating Mir in the second round, Lesnar shouted disparaging remarks about the evening's beer sponsor, made sexual innuendos regarding his own wife and gave the crowd the middle finger. His actions went viral. UFC 100 ranks as the biggest UFC pay-per-view event of all time — eclipsing 1.6 million buys — and the media storm following the bout forced pundits to question whether Lesnar's actions were good for the sport. What can't be debated: he is the perfect showman, a love him or hate him kind of guy whose larger-than-life personality injected a much-needed dose of energy into the heavyweight division and the UFC at large, propelling the discussion beyond the confines of the octagon and into the bedrooms of the American public.

Sidelined by a serious case of diverticulitis (a digestive disease), it took a year for Lesnar to prove he could defend his belt. But he returned in 2010 with a vengeance. His fight against Shane Carwin at UFC 116 proved two more things: he could take some damage — as evidenced by a first round that saw Carwin throw all he had at Lesnar's granite chin — and he could carry a card on his own. The UFC's bottom line received a huge boost with his return, and UFC 116 ranks as the second-highest PPV audience ever. In fact, four of the top-10 all-time best-selling fights had Lesnar on the card.

Four months later, Cain Velasquez overthrew Lesnar to claim the belt. Health issues continued to plague the big man, and in late 2011, his fight versus Alistair Overeem turned out to be his last. After having a 12-inch piece of his colon removed to deal with his disease, Lesnar simply wasn't the same, succumbing to tough shots to his midsection and strong kicks from the former kickboxing champion, resulting in a first-round stoppage. He announced his retirement after the fight.

Lesnar finished his MMA career with a 5-3 record, but he's not done competing yet. He is once again a superstar in WWE, fighting in high-profile matches like Wrestlemania XXX. He wasn't the UFC's greatest heavyweight, nor the most politically correct, but his impact on the sport is undeniable. He brought a much-needed dose of superstar power into the promotion, and for that, his legacy remains intact.

TALE OF THE TAPE

BORN

UNITED STATES

D.O.B.
1977/07/12

HEIGHT
6'3"

WEIGHT
266 lb.

ASSOCIATION
Team Death Clutch

NICKNAME
N/A

Above: Quinton Jackson tags Dan Henderson with a thunderous right during his victory at UFC 75. Right: Jackson knocks out Chuck Liddell at UFC 71 for the light heavyweight championship.

WITH HIS MENACING grimace, heavy right hand and Hollywood-like persona, Quinton "Rampage" Jackson, the UFC's former light heavyweight champion, is a larger-than-life character who has transcended the sport to become a must-see attraction no matter what arena he is in.

Jackson's career began in low-level promotions throughout the United States, where the high school wrestler posted a 10-1 record. When he arrived in Japan to fight for Pride in 2001, the 6-foot-1, 205-pound Jackson was an instant fan favorite and a

novelty as an African-American fighting in the country. He dabbled in kickboxing but settled on MMA, where he went 9-2 over a three-year period, defeating an array of tough men, including Igor Vovchanchyn, Kevin Randleman and Chuck Liddell.

One of Jackson's greatest adversaries was Wanderlei "the Axe Murderer" Silva. They first met in Tokyo in 2003, a tournament-style bout that saw Jackson taste defeat at the hands of the Brazilian. They met again one year later at Pride 28, an all-out war in which Silva captured the Pride middleweight title by violently knocking out Rampage with a barrage of knees. It was a devastating finish, and not one Jackson soon forgot.

He kept battling though. His most impressive Pride win came against Ricardo Arona. The Brazilian utilized many tough leg kicks to chop down Rampage. "Arona had the hardest kicks I've ever felt in my life," said Jackson. Arona even dislocated Jackson's jaw, and believing the American to be knocked out, he mentioned this to the referee. Bad idea. Jackson's temper boiled, and when Arona later caught him in a triangle choke, Rampage lifted his opponent up and body-slammed him to the mat, knocking Arona unconscious. It went down as one of the most memorable moments in the history of the promotion.

Jackson wasn't quite a household name when he came back to the United States to fight in the UFC. "My family didn't even know I was in Japan," he joked in 2008. But for a guy from Memphis, who'd grown up poor and with little contact from a drug-addled father, his homecoming was sweet.

In only his second UFC fight, Jackson landed a title shot versus Chuck Liddell, who was riding a seven-fight winning streak. Liddell's last career loss had been to Rampage in Pride in 2003. Since then Liddell had become a popular UFC champion, and he wanted nothing more than to avenge his loss. He wouldn't get redemption that night, however, as Jackson KO'd the UFC's darling in the first round with a powerful overhand right to steal away the light heavyweight crown.

Jackson unified the Pride and UFC belts with a win over Dan Henderson, but a misstep versus Forrest Griffin cost him his title. He'd make up for it, but it wouldn't be against Griffin. On December 27, 2008, Jackson and his old nemesis Silva met for the third and final time at UFC 92 to complete their storied trilogy. Wearing his trademark industrial chain around his neck— a gimmick that started in high school wrestling to bump a losing streak — Jackson entered the Las Vegas arena that night on a mission. It was

his first fight since losing the belt, and he had switched coaches, moving to London to train. The renewed focus paid off, and Rampage exacted his revenge on Silva, connecting with a hard left hook to the Brazilian's jaw — "on the button," according to Joe Rogan during the broadcast — and the man who'd caused the Memphis-born fighter so much grief was out cold at 3:21 of the first round.

Hollywood came knocking, and soon Rampage debuted on the silver screen, starring as B.A. Baracus in the 2010 film *The A-Team*. After two coaching stints on *The Ultimate Fighter*, it was obvious Rampage had the chops to straddle the roles of both entertainer and fighter, but his relationship with the UFC became strained (he claims it was ever since he knocked out Liddell). He'd finish his contract, but Jackson's best days were behind him. He left on a three-fight losing streak, a new wave of talent like Jon Jones and Ryan Bader simply too much. But he wasn't done fighting, and joined Bellator where he won his first three bouts. And he could still stir the pot; at Bellator 120 in 2014, Rampage was fined $10,000 for shoving Muhammed Lawal at the weigh-ins, before scoring a unanimous decision for the win.

Always an entertaining quote, a natural showman and a fierce competitor, Rampage's legacy, no matter where he fights, will be as one of the most unique characters to ever step into the octagon.

TALE OF
THE TAPE

BORN

UNITED STATES

D.O.B.
1978/06/20

HEIGHT
6'1"

WEIGHT
205 lb.

ASSOCIATION
Wolfslair
Academy

NICKNAME
Rampage

RASHAD EVANS

Above: Rashad Evans scores a split-decision victory over Dan Henderson in their light heavyweight fight at UFC 161 in 2013. Right: Evans scores Knockout of the Night at UFC 88 in his light heavyweight bout against Chuck Liddell.

RAISED ON THE border town of Niagara Falls, New York, in a single-parent family of eight kids, Rashad Evans, a high school football and wrestling champion, rose through the ranks, landing at Michigan State where he earned a psychology degree and established himself as one of the best wrestlers in his weight class. Studying karate at a young age, Evans — nicknamed "Suga" — was a natural when he added MMA to his resume. Over the past decade, he's put together a world-class UFC career that includes the title of light heavyweight champion.

Evans' stint on *The Ultimate Fighter 2* launched his career. He won seven straight fights to earn a spot on the burgeoning reality show on Spike TV, the cast of which featured both welterweights and heavyweights. Evans earned an early rep on the program as a showboat, but he proved he could back up his antics, defeating Brad Imes to win the competition and secure a UFC contract.

Suga shed some weight and scrapped at light heavyweight to begin his UFC tenure, fighting out of famed coach Greg Jackson's camp. Already 8-0, the 5-foot-11, 205-pounder rattled off four victories, including a Knockout of the Night versus Sean Salmon, before facing his toughest challenge yet.

Tito Ortiz was the king of the hill when it came to spewing venom, but Evans had a mouth that could trash-talk with the best of them. He called out Ortiz before their UFC 73 bout, bristling the star by labeling him a "poser" and an "entertainer." Ortiz, coming off a title fight with Chuck Liddell, was immensely popular; Evans was still trying to prove his worth. His base takeaway for UFC 73 was just $16,000. The 2007 fight was a takedown-heavy match that ended in a draw because of a point deduction against Ortiz. Evans' ability to hang in with one of the big boys of the promotion was enough to propel him to the big stage.

A subsequent win versus Michael Bisping secured a bout with Liddell at UFC 88 and Evans didn't disappoint, destroying the former champ in the second round with a KO heard around the world. It established Suga as the top challenger in the division, earning him a title shot versus Forrest Griffin. Evans pounded Griffin into submission, winning the belt at 2:46 of the third round to end 2008 with a bang. In 16 MMA fights, Evans hadn't posted a loss, and he began 2009 as the undisputed light heavyweight champion of the world.

His reign would last just six months. A poor matchup versus Brazilian Lyoto Machida ended abruptly in the second round, as the counterpunching karate fighter stopped the cocky American in his tracks with a flurry of punches. Unanimous wins in 2010 against Thiago Silva and Rampage Jackson — both six-figure paydays — and a thunderous TKO of Ortiz in their rematch at UFC 133 the next year catapulted Evans to another title shot. But it would be against an unlikely opponent.

Evans never wanted to fight Jon Jones. He had taken the younger Jones under his wing at Greg Jackson's camp in New Mexico, but things soured between the two fighters when Jones accepted a title bout that likely would have gone to Evans had he not been injured at the time. Not only that, when the

upstart upset Mauricio "Shogun" Rua in that title fight, he said he'd fight Evans if the UFC asked him to. Evans, feeling disrespected, left Jackson's tutelage and joined "the Blackzilians" in Florida. When the friends turned foes finally met at UFC 145, Dana White summed it up by saying, "This is the fight business, not the friend business." Any existing bad blood didn't surface during the fight, and Jones used his reach and sound strategy to keep Evans at bay. Evans was respectful after the loss. "He was creative and kept me on my toes," he said. "I've got to give it up to him."

At 24-3-1, Evans has been a staple in the UFC the last decade. He's ninth all time in total fight time and sixth in takedowns landed. His knockout power may be latent of late, but above-average takedown and strike defense over his career has kept him in the mix. Since the failed title bid against Jones, he's turned a corner with recent wins over Dan Henderson and Chael Sonnen. Another injury will sideline Evans for most of 2014, but he remains a perennial headliner and strong draw at the box office. One of the best light heavyweights around, with another convincing win, his return to glory may be just one punch away.

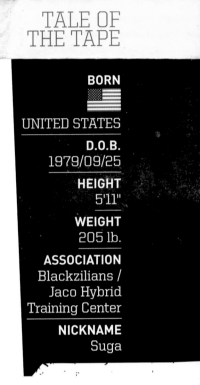

TALE OF THE TAPE

BORN

UNITED STATES

D.O.B.
1979/09/25

HEIGHT
5'11"

WEIGHT
205 lb.

ASSOCIATION
Blackzilians /
Jaco Hybrid
Training Center

NICKNAME
Suga

Team Canada fighter Kajan Johnson defeats Team Australia fighter Brendan O'Reilly in their welterweight bout during the filming of *The Ultimate Fighter Nations* on November 2, 2013.

MMA, THE INTERNET AND MAINSTREAM ACCEPTANCE

SINCE THE INCEPTION of the Ultimate Fighting Championship in 1993, mixed martial arts has grown at an unprecedented pace, transitioning from a stigmatized, somewhat illegal sport that many viewed as a violent freak show to one of the fastest-growing spectator sports in the world. The reason for its initial popularity? The Internet.

For early fans and adopters of MMA, there was very little coverage of mixed martial arts bouts in the 1990s. Diehard fans could buy tickets and attend events, and a modest number

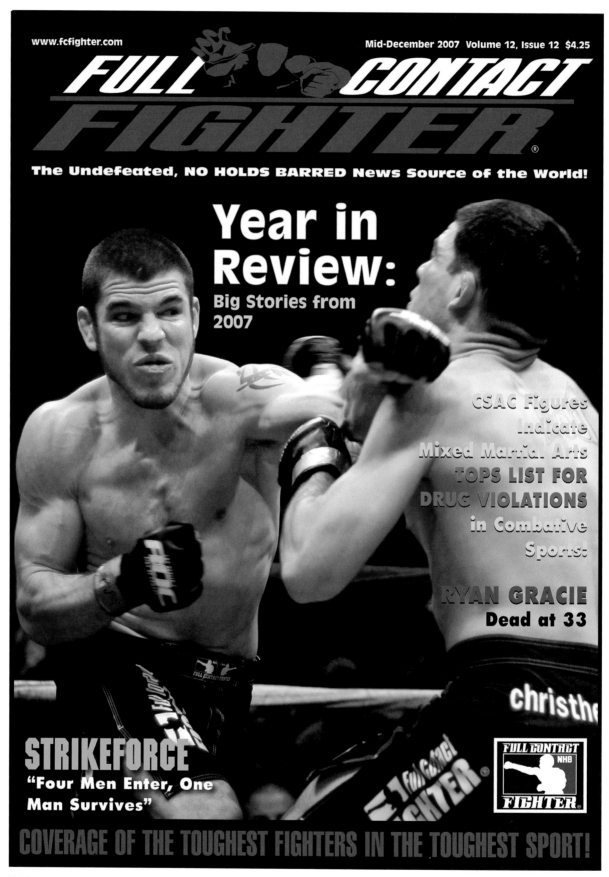

Full Contact Fighter, the first publication devoted solely to MMA.

of others saw fights live through obscure pay-per-view stations, as the UFC had essentially been blacklisted by the major cable and satellite companies. Some smaller publications such as the monthly *Full Contact Fighter* covered the sport, but no major newspapers or television networks covered MMA events. Without the Internet, elite-level MMA would have essentially taken place in a vacuum.

By the late 1990s the Internet had become accessible to most people, and it alone became the only consistent source for fight fans to find information on MMA and its top stars. Young entrepreneurs like Jeff Sherwood (www.sherdog.com), Joel Gold (www.fullcontactfighter.com) and Ryan Bennett (www.mmaweekly.com) created vibrant websites through hard work and a passion for the sport.

Sherwood, an avid photographer, began his website in the mid-1990s while he was working in California for the airline manufacturer Boeing. He never imagined the site would draw much of a following, so he simply used his nickname, Sherdog, to create the first site: Sherdog's UFC Fan Page. "When I first started this site I was simply a fan," explained Sherwood. "I wasn't a journalist, but at the beginning . . . I thought my job was to cover the sport's history." Originally the website published fight results and matchups for upcoming events. In 1999 Sherwood posted his first interview: Bas Rutten. The Dutch star opened up to Sherdog, speaking on a variety of topics, including a story about how he would toughen up his shins by kicking telephone poles. The piece was a huge success.

The site's scope grew slowly and steadily until Sherwood brought in Garrett Poe to help. Poe was studying polymer science and engineering at the University of Southern Mississippi, and he made mixed martial arts videos in his spare time. "[Poe's videos] could make my website huge," Sherwood recalls thinking at the time. And he was right. Once the videos were posted, the site exploded in popularity.

Later www.sherdog.com became the first website to create a fighter database. It was a labor of love for Sherwood and his staff. Over the years they've put in countless hours, recording fighter information and match results. Currently Sherwood's database is the catalogue of record, and it has information on over 10,000 events and 42,000 fighters. There are many imitators, but only one original.

Kirik Jenness and Gabe Smallman started their website — www.submissionfighting.com (now www.mixed-martialarts.com) — in 1998. Both men were avid Brazilian jiu-jitsu practitioners and felt there was a need to provide people with news about the sport. Early on the partners realized that people were struggling to find out about martial arts schools, or basic information about training options, so they decided to create an open forum for their visitors to interact. "Around then we found an online forum about self-defence," said Smallman. "And Kirik said, 'I wish we had something like this' so I built a little forum from a sample code I got out of a book and it kept growing."

This was the genesis of what later became known as "The Underground," for many years the most popular mixed martial arts forum in the world. The Underground's popularity is due to the fact that many of the biggest names in the sport are regular contributors to the discussion. UFC CEO Lorenzo Fertitta, former UFC champion Tito Ortiz and fighter/manager Monte Cox are all members, and each engages in online discussions with fans and experts. And Kirik is a tough monitor. "I have banned thousands of members who couldn't post about a fighter as if they were speaking to that fighter's face," he says. "I have tried for a decade to improve a place that the sport's most passionate devotees, fans, and fighters alike, are comfortable with."

In Queens, New York, Joel Gold is the man behind *Full Contact Fighter*, a newspaper he has been publishing since 1997 (it is now also a website). Like Sherwood, Gold was a photographer who built his publication around photographs and event results. Even then, it was difficult to turn a profit in the newspaper business, so Gold looked at ancillary revenue streams to bring in money. One of the first he tapped into was the seemingly insatiable demand fight fans had for VHS tapes and, later, DVDs. Through sites like Sherdog, fans became aware of the many different promotions around the world (such as Pancrase and Pride in Japan). With this awareness came a demand to see the events, and entrepreneurs like Gold were able to negotiate deals with the various event rights holders to sell tapes and DVDs through their media outlets — a slam dunk.

Full Contact Fighter also developed a clothing line to service the demands of the small but loyal group of fans who were following the sport and wanted to identify themselves with it. They began selling T-shirts, hats and hoodies with the Full Contact Fighter brand. This side of the business eventually became Full Contact Fighter's most profitable area, and it wouldn't be long before others were getting in on the wearable merchandise craze.

In 1997 three friends, Charles "Mask" Lewis, Dan "Punkass" Caldwell, and Tim "SkyScrape" Katz formed TapouT to sell mixed martial arts clothing and accessories. All three had trained in MMA and understood what their customers wanted, because they wanted it too. Lewis recalls how he felt after his first purchase of a mixed martial arts T-shirt after a class with the legendary Royce Gracie. "I walked out after my private lesson, bought a Gracie jiu-jitsu T-shirt, and bro, if you told me to fight Mike Tyson, I'd have been like 'I'm gonna take him down and the fight'll be over. And he needs to worry about it because I'm wearing a Gracie T-shirt.' That's where it started." The trio parlayed this passion into a multimillion-dollar company. By 2009, TapouT registered over $200 million in sales, making it one of the world's top sports apparel companies.

Today, along with clothing lines by Hayabusa, Affliction, Bad Boy and others, many apparel companies have made small fortunes tapping into the fervent loyalty and pride of MMA fans. Unlike traditional sports, where team uniforms identify fans to other likeminded individuals, MMA clothing companies helped create a visual, wearable culture for those eager to let the rest of the world know they are part of the MMA tribe.

Indeed, the clothing folks can take some credit for the growth of MMA, and without the Internet, it is certain the sport may not have made its way out of the 1990s with such a strong stride. But when it comes down to it, the credit for the rapid expansion of MMA in the following decade should go to the one medium that has proven time and time again to be crucial in fostering mainstream acceptance — television.

When the UFC decided to invest in *The Ultimate Fighter* — paying the production costs so it could air on the Spike channel in 2005 — it was the last big investment Lorenzo Fertitta and his brother and business partner, Frank, were willing to make into the promotion they had purchased five years earlier. In its first season, *The Ultimate Fighter* featured a plethora of future stars, including Forrest Griffin, Chris Leben and Stephan Bonnar. All participants were coached by one of two legends, either Randy Couture or Chuck Liddell. The series ended with an all-out slugfest between Griffin and Bonnar that was broadcast live on Spike. *TUF* was a smash hit and is still on the air to this day. The format is so successful that it has been used in other countries around the world such as Canada, Australia, the United Kingdom, Brazil and China.

Tim "SkyScrape" Katz (left) and Dan "Punkass" Caldwell of TapouT pose after winning the Best Lifestyle Clothing Brand award at the Fighters Only World Mixed Martial Arts Awards in 2011.

The impact of *The Ultimate Fighter* cannot be overstated. At the time it debuted, Spike TV was seen in almost 100 million homes. The series marked the first time mixed martial arts had reached so many people on a weekly basis. Out of the success of *The Ultimate Fighter*, the Fertittas and UFC president Dana White were able to market the UFC brand to the masses, create new stars each year from the series, and leverage the show's audience reach to promote rising stars and upcoming pay-per-views. Historically, it's clear that the sport's popularity skyrocketed after the show debuted, which ultimately turned the Chuck Liddells and Randy Coutures of the world into mainstream personalities (Liddell's fame was such that he was invited to participate on Dancing with the Stars, and Randy Couture has since appeared in numerous Hollywood blockbusters). The UFC, of course, reaped the benefit of *TUF*'s success, as did the fighters. And for companies like TapouT and websites like Sherdog, the passion and hard work of building something from nothing was rewarded with the next wave of MMA's growth. It is a rags-to-riches story as true as they come, and today, there are a few leaders from the media and the business world that are keeping it going.

MEDIA MOVERS AND SHAKERS

MIKE GOLDBERG

Mike Goldberg has been doing play-by-play for the UFC since 1997 and has called more important MMA title fights than any other commentator in history. Originally, he was the voice of NHL games for ESPN before he got his opportunity with the UFC. His producer at the time, Bruce Connell, also produced UFC events and suggested Goldberg give the fledging sport a try. "I didn't get my [hockey] contract renewed in Detroit and at about the same time Bruce Beck [original UFC play-by-play man] left the UFC to take a full time job with NBC in New York," Goldberg said. "Bruce called me and said that he had a gig for me, it was in Japan, it's in December and that I had to take a jiu-jitsu class."

Goldberg immediately solidified his role with the UFC and has been a fixture at almost every major UFC event for 17 years. His success enticed World Wrestling Entertainment to offer him a huge contract to leave the UFC and join them as the lead commentator on their flagship show, *RAW*. They even offered him a six-figure bonus to "no-show" at an upcoming UFC event. To his credit, Goldberg turned down the offer, did the UFC event and never looked back, becoming the UFC's iconic voice.

ARIEL HELWANI

Canadian journalist Ariel Helwani has established himself as the toughest interviewer in MMA. Using his popular podcast, *MMA Hour*, Helwani's developed a huge following by asking tough questions while still being diplomatic enough to keep regular access to some of the biggest names in the sport. In other words, he has consistently come across as someone who loves the sport but rarely throws softball questions to the biggest names in the business. His interviews with personalities like Bob Sapp, Rampage Jackson and Nick Diaz are legendary and helped earn Helwani MMA Journalist of the Year from 2010 through 2013 at the World MMA Awards. "If I'm scared of someone getting mad at me for asking a question then I shouldn't be in this business," he said. "I don't get guys getting mad at me because these guys get it. These guys are very open. That's what I love about this sport."

At the time he began his career as an MMA journalist he told himself he wanted to be the Howard Cosell of mixed martial arts broadcasting. When Fox Sports hired him as a reporter, Helwani could finally say he reached the same huge audiences that his hero had in the 1960s and '70s working for ABC Sports. "I like to think I tell it like it is," Helwani said. "I learned that from Howard Cosell — that was his catchphrase."

DAVE MELTZER

Although Dave Meltzer is best known for his *Wrestling Observer* newsletter, a bible for pro wrestling fans, he is also one of the longest serving and most respected mixed martial arts writers. For the past two decades Meltzer has dedicated a section of his newsletter to MMA. Through his pro wrestling contacts, he has been able to present fairly accurate pay-per-view numbers and is often cited as a source by other writers who are covering the business side of the sport.

His writing has also been important to the sport because of his willingness and ability to cover mixed

Left: UFC play-by-play announcer Mike Goldberg addresses the audience prior to UFC on Fox 11. Right: Ariel Helwani interviews Dan Henderson during the UFC 173 Ultimate Media Day.

martial arts promotions in other countries. For example, the *Wrestling Observer* newsletter has long been the only place MMA fans could read in-depth reports on events like the now defunct Rings promotion from Japan or the infamous IVC events from Brazil.

The thoroughness and quality of his MMA reporting and analysis are unmatched despite the fact that MMA is really the second sport he covers beyond professional wrestling. Frank Deford of *Sports Illustrated*, acknowledged as one of the greatest sports writers of all time, calls Meltzer "the most accomplished reporter in sports journalism."

JEFF SHERWOOD

The unassuming Jeff Sherwood is a true mixed martial arts pioneer and one of the key figures in keeping the sport alive during its difficult years in the late 1990s. He freely admits to not being much of a writer and confesses to not having a great understanding of computer technology, yet he has an incredible understanding of what fans of the sport want from their media sources.

In addition to his website, www.sherdog.com, Sherwood created the Sherdog Radio Network, which is host to some of MMA's most popular web-only audio programs — *The Savage Dog Show*, *Beatdown*, *It's Time* and *The Jordan Breen Show*.

Perhaps the most notable accomplishment is Sherdog's relationship with the biggest sports media entity in the world, ESPN. Sherdog provides MMA information for visitors to the ESPN site as well as access to Sherdog's Fight Finder. The site also live-streams a large number of mixed martial arts events like Palace Fighting Championship, War Dogs, and M-1 Global.

BUSINESS POWER PLAYERS

LORENZO FERTITTA

UFC CEO and chairman Lorenzo Fertitta may prefer to let his friend and partner Dana White make most of the UFC's public pronouncements, but that shouldn't take away from the immense contributions he has made to the growth of mixed martial arts and the UFC.

Unlike White, whose major business accomplishment is the UFC itself, Fertitta had already proven himself in the business world by the time he took over the promotion. He, along with brother Frank, ran Station Casinos and oversaw real estate and other investments, including the Gordon Biersch beer company.

Additionally, Fertitta developed important relationships

when he held the titles of Nevada Athletic Commissioner and the chairman of the Nevada Resort Association. These proved invaluable when it came time to seek sanctioning for the UFC in Nevada and other states.

Although Fertitta tries to keep a low profile — spending a great deal of time working on the company's international expansion — there are times when he will represent the company to the media, and in those instances, his professional, businesslike persona can be much more effective than Dana White's bombastic and, at times, defensive approach to tough questioning from the media.

BJORN REBNEY

Since creating Bellator Fighting Championships (now called Bellator Mixed Martial Arts) in 2008, Bjorn Rebney has guided his promotion to become North America's second most powerful fighting organization by virtue of two brilliant strategic decisions.

First, Bellator events are mainly tournament based, with the winners earning a shot at the current champion in each weight group. It's a brilliant concept that was used very effectively by early UFC promoters. It's a strategy that Rebney feels takes the power away from himself, placing it in the hands of the fighters. "It's the way that sport is supposed to work," he said. "Sport is about competition. Sport is about everyone having a chance to win."

The second move Rebney made to establish Bellator's strong position in the North American market was to convince the massive media company Viacom to buy a majority stake in

his company. The deal with Viacom gives Bellator an owner with tremendous resources and has made the promotion a flagship program on Spike TV, the original carrier of the UFC's *The Ultimate Fighter*. "Spike basically wrote the book on mixed martial arts," said Rebney. "Spike is the network where MMA fans live."

Under Rebney's leadership Bellator has been broadcast for 10 seasons and is seen in the United States, Canada, Russia, the Middle East, Asia and Australia, and season 1 of its own reality show, *Fight Masters*, recently debuted.

JOE SILVA

UFC matchmaker Joe Silva is the man most responsible for the organization's product. "Dana [White] is Captain Kirk and we're Scotty," he once said, referring to himself and his matchmaking partner, Sean Shelby. "Dana's always asking for impossible stuff and we're saying we can't do it!"

Essentially, Silva and Shelby create the product. There is an art to the role. They need to create not only an entertaining fight but also a matchup that fans think will be entertaining — otherwise they won't buy tickets.

Silva may play down his capabilities, but he's been the

one person who has been a part of nearly every UFC main event fight ever. His relationship and role with the company extend all the way back into the 1990s before the promotion was owned by the Fertitta brothers. He endeared himself to former UFC owner Bob Meyrowitz by demonstrating an encyclopedic knowledge of fighters thanks to countless hours watching DVDs and VHS tapes.

Although Silva is rarely heard from on the radio, the Internet or television, he does wield an extraordinary amount of power within the UFC. As Dana White so eloquently explains to his fighters, "If you call Joe Silva and you turn down a fight, you might as well rip up your contract."

DANA WHITE

In 15 years, controversial and confrontational UFC president Dana White has turned a company and sport that was near death into the biggest sports success story of our time.

Under his leadership the UFC received sanctioning, was put back on pay-per-view cable and satellite television, produced a hit TV show in *The Ultimate Fighter* and turned an initial $3 million investment into a multibillion-dollar enterprise.

One of the conscious decisions White made, along with the Fertittas, was to make himself the biggest star in the UFC. Part of the reason was that communication and promotion became easy when the promoter himself was the person the media went to when a question needed to be answered. The other reason? It meant that as business owners, the three of them would never be put in a position where a fighter had more power than they did.

White's personality and leadership style supported this approach. He's engaged in public feuds with everyone from boxing promoter Bob Arum to UFC champions like Randy Couture, Tito Ortiz and Ken Shamrock. It's an oppositional style that one could say is consistent with his often violent product and has worked far better than anyone, except White, could ever have imagined.

Below: Dana White engages with fans prior to UFC 168: Weidman v Silva 2.
Left: Bellator founder and CEO, Bjorn Rebney, attends the postfight press conference at Bellator 39 in 2011.

Johny Hendricks enters the arena before UFC 171. Hendricks defeated Robbie Lawler to capture the welterweight title for the first time.

RISING STARS

Above: Johny Hendricks lands one of his many punches on Georges St-Pierre at UFC 167. St-Pierre retained his title, but the victory was marred by controversy. Right: Hendricks blocks a kick from Martin Kampmann at UFC 154. Hendricks knocked out Kampmann at 0:46 of the first round.

THEY CALL HIM "Bigg Rigg." It's a fitting name for a compact power puncher from Oklahoma, a people's kind of guy whose rise through the welterweight ranks has been a steady ascent to the top, sprinkled with just a little adversity. And along the way, Johny Hendricks, the four-time All-America wrestler and two-time national winner armed with a knockout left, became a champion, proving that hard work, dedication and a willingness to stay the course end in triumph.

Early UFC wins over T.J. Grant and Charlie Brenneman proved Hendricks was capable of handling midlevel competition among the welterweight division. But his first loss as a pro to Rick Story in *The Ultimate Fighter 12* finale knocked Hendricks down a peg, forcing the Oklahoma native to fight his way up again versus lesser-knowns.

The 30-year-old southpaw with the trademark bushy beard has averaged 4.25 takedowns per fight in the UFC, relying early in his career on superior wrestling. But his knockout power became the talk of the town when he dropped fellow wrestler Jon Fitch in just 12 seconds at UFC 141 in late 2011.

The following year, Hendricks ended Martin Kampmann's evening at 46 seconds of the first round. The two knockouts opened the UFC brass up to the possibility that Hendricks could be a viable contender for Georges St-Pierre's belt. But first, Bigg Rigg would need to defeat Carlos Condit, a perennial top-5 member of the welterweight class, which he did at UFC 158 in early 2013 in front of St-Pierre's hometown crowd of Montreal. The stage was set: Hendricks would face the French-Canadian at UFC 167 in what would become one of the most controversial decisions in UFC history.

For five rounds the two fighters battered each other. The first was nearly even. But Hendricks took it to the champ in round two. St-Pierre looked worse for wear, his face bloodied and bruised. Hendricks, more than any man during the French-Canadian's reign, was causing him serious damage. But St-Pierre fought back gamely in round three, with Hendricks inflicting more wear and tear in the fourth. By the end of the fifth and final round, despite advanced statistics illustrating that Hendricks had outstruck his opponent mightily throughout the bout, St-Pierre narrowly escaped with a split decision. "The judges kind of ripped my heart out," Hendricks said after the fight. Dana White expressed frustration with the Nevada State Commission, stating, "I'm blown away that Georges St-Pierre won that fight, and . . . I'm a promoter."

There is a maxim in mixed martial arts: to beat the champ, you have to win convincingly. Although Hendricks made a strong case for the belt that night, it wasn't a surefire knockout or five rounds of complete domination. He would have to wait, like he always has, for a shot at redemption. Only it wouldn't be against St-Pierre, who vacated the belt at the end of 2013. Hendricks would have to go to war one more time to achieve immortality.

UFC 171 in March 2014: the first time a new welterweight champion would be crowned in seven years. Standing opposite Hendricks: Robbie Lawler, once a rising star who had climbed back into contention with notable victories in 2013 over top-10 contenders Rory MacDonald and Josh Koscheck. Prior to the fight, Reebok gambled and signed the affable Hendricks to a sponsorship contract, the first UFC member on their roster. Hendricks didn't disappoint.

Standing in the pocket all night, both men traded heavy blows in the most strike-heavy title fight in UFC history. An early lead for Hendricks evaporated in the third and fourth rounds, as Lawler proved his heart was as mighty as his fists. If not for a well-executed takedown in the final round, Hendricks may have lost. But Bigg Rigg came out on top, falling joyfully to the mat when Dana White wrapped the belt around his waist.

Amassing a 16-2 record, Hendricks is entering a new phase of his career, one where potential challengers are calling him out for a shot at the belt. He'll be shelved for the majority of 2014, however, having torn his biceps muscle in his victory over Lawler.

Thanks to winning the belt, Hendricks will not only see a pay increase every time he fights but also rake in the real money: marketing dollars. With St-Pierre out of the picture, Hendricks has proven, like the tortoise, that his slow and steady ascent was able to win the race. He just happened to have a powerful left hand to go along with the indomitable spirit of the tortoise.

TALE OF THE TAPE

BORN

🇺🇸

UNITED STATES

D.O.B.
1983/09/12

HEIGHT
5'9"

WEIGHT
170 lb.

ASSOCIATION
Team Takedown

NICKNAME
Bigg Rigg

RORY MacDONALD

Above: Rory MacDonald tags Demian Maia with a hard overhand right at UFC 170. MacDonald was awarded a unanimous-decision victory. Right: MacDonald throws Nate Diaz en route to victory at UFC 129.

ARES, THE GOD of war and son of Zeus in Greek mythology, is a nickname fit for any fighter. But for Canadian welterweight Rory MacDonald, the name carries extra meaning. Cast early on as the heir to the 170-pound throne — held for seven years by Georges St-Pierre — it appears "Ares" is well on his way to following in his mentor's footsteps and challenging for the right to be called a god among men.

Don't let MacDonald's shy, reserved demeanor outside the octagon deceive you. As well-rounded a fighter as they come,

MacDonald morphs into a ruthless, violent mixed martial artist when he steps into the ring. The welterweight's been a phenom since a young age, when as a skinny 14-year-old growing up in Kelowna, British Columbia, he walked into David Lea's gym, Toshido, and started training, eventually taking on bigger, stronger teenagers who couldn't slip one by the kid. By 16, he was winning bouts throughout western Canada. By 20, he was the youngest fighter in the UFC.

At UFC 115 in Vancouver in 2010, MacDonald suited up for just his second

UFC fight. His opponent? Future interim welterweight champion Carlos Condit, a polished striker from Albuquerque, New Mexico, with an arsenal of dangerous kicks and strong Brazilian jiu-jitsu. Sporting a buzz cut, MacDonald looked every bit the boy just out of high school. Coming off a submission win against Mike Guymon, the Canadian was brimming with confidence. "He's still a man. He still can be defeated," MacDonald said in a prefight interview. And he nearly did so in front of a hometown crowd. For two rounds, Ares offered a series of punches and knees to Condit's body, dominating the older fighter. Round three was a different story: Condit wailed down strikes and elbows on the hapless rookie, opening up a severe cut on MacDonald's face. The referee, Kevin Dornan, stopped the scrap with just seven seconds left. Both men earned Fight of the Night honors and a bonus check, cementing the Canuck's status as a future star in the organization.

MacDonald didn't follow up the contentious Condit loss by sulking. Using his 6-foot frame and 76-inch reach, he disposed of veteran after veteran — Nate Diaz, Mike Pyle, Che Mills — appearing hungrier and hungrier, culminating in a much-hyped fight with former two-time belt holder and UFC legend BJ Penn. The young stud demolished the aging vet, pummeling Penn for much of their 15 minutes in the ring. Talk of MacDonald vying for a title shot was beginning to grow. But welterweight champion St-Pierre was vocal — he and MacDonald, training partners and close friends at Tristar Gym in Montreal — would never fight.

Following the Penn bout, MacDonald came down to earth after skyrocketing up the welterweight ranks. In July 2013, he narrowly escaped with a win against top-ranked Jake Ellenberger, but the fight barely registered on the Richter scale — a total dud from start to finish. Despite a strong jab that kept Ellenberger at a distance, MacDonald was criticized for playing it safe. Even the UFC brass wasn't happy with the scrap. "That fight sucked so bad," president Dana White said in a postfight press conference. "Rory's one of the best in the world. He didn't look it tonight."

MacDonald followed up with another disappointing fight, only his second career loss, this time to Robbie Lawler, a scrappy puncher who overtook a less aggressive MacDonald in the later rounds. "I needed to lose," MacDonald told Ariel Helwani's radio show, *The MMA Hour*, after the fight. "I'm very motivated now. I feel like I have that fire back." Entering the ring for the third time in seven months at the beginning of 2014, MacDonald registered an important come-from-behind victory versus top-10 welterweight Demian Maia, and then reasserted himself in the discussion of top 170-pound fighters with a one-sided win over Tyron Woodley in front of his hometown fans at UFC 174 in June 2014.

With St-Pierre inching closer to officially retiring, the welterweight division has never been more wide open. Fighters champing at the bit to assert their dominance are at an all-time high, and young, established names like MacDonald need that fire if they're going to rise up the ranks. With a 17-2 record, Ares is no slouch. When you're named after the son of the mightiest god in all of mythology, it's a lot to carry on your shoulders. But with youth on his side, the hardest lessons are behind him. Watch out. We may be watching the evolution of a future champion.

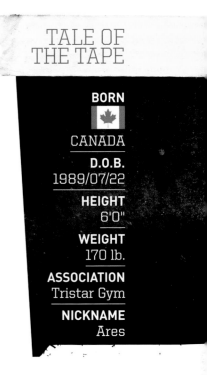

TALE OF THE TAPE

BORN
🇨🇦
CANADA

D.O.B.
1989/07/22

HEIGHT
6'0"

WEIGHT
170 lb.

ASSOCIATION
Tristar Gym

NICKNAME
Ares

DUSTIN POIRIER

Above: Dustin Poirier hammers Cub Swanson in their featherweight fight at UFC on Fuel TV 7. Right: Poirier kicks Diego Brandao at UFC 168. The win at UFC 168 was his second after his disappointing loss to Swanson.

A DIAMOND IS the hardest known mineral in the world. Formed 100 miles below the surface, diamonds, made of carbon, are subject to searing heat and mounting pressure from the earth above and the rock below. These billion-year-old carbon atoms bond together to create something unlike anything else in the world. And maybe, just maybe, Dustin "the Diamond" Poirier is on track to emerge from the pressure of his life to become his own unique gem.

As the focal point of the 2011 documentary *Fightville*, it was obvious Poirier possessed something special. At the outset of the film, the Lafayette, Louisiana, native is introduced as an aspiring MMA fighter. A tough kid from an even tougher background — he constantly found himself scrapping in the schoolyard — Poirier turned to boxing and mixed martial arts as a way to channel his misguided energy. "I needed this in my life," he says about MMA in the film. "It's given me discipline and focus." That's included keeping his weight down by avoiding ice cream and sticking to a healthy diet of tuna, quinoa and organic coconut butter when training.

Suffice it to say, just five years after filming began, the UFC featherweight is no longer on the rise, he's arrived — with a fury. Equipped with an indomitable work ethic and a fierce competitive spirit honed from those childhood brawls, Poirier's 16-3 record includes six submission wins. With his 73-inch reach and southpaw stance, the 25-year-old rattled off four straight victories to begin his UFC career, capping off his unbeaten streak with a Submission of the Night victory versus Max Holloway and garnering an extra $65,000 in bonus money. But this isn't what ultimately put Poirier on the radar as a legitimate talent.

His fifth fight, UFC on Fuel TV: Korean Zombie vs. Poirier, has been Poirier's biggest and most famous to date — and it was a barn burner. Alternating between a standup brawl and technique-driven match on the ground with multiple submission attempts, the energetic scrap went back and forth for three rounds, with Poirier bloody but not beaten. In the fourth round, Poirier eventually lost to a D'Arce choke from the Zombie (Chan Sung Jung), but both fighters picked up Fight of the Night honors, and Sherdog, ESPN and MMAFighting.com called it the Fight of the Year in 2012. The fight established the featherweight as both a resilient, hard-nosed competitor and a household name in MMA.

Poirier alternated wins and losses in 2012–13, but strictly evaluating him in the win column misses the point. His fights always provide entertainment value, and even in his loss to Cub Swanson at UFC on Fuel TV 7, Poirier mixed a variety of leg kicks, takedown attempts and strong striking skills to combat Swanson's well-rounded, hard-hitting attack. (Poirier averages 4.45 significant strikes landed per minute, compared with 3.13 absorbed in the UFC.) Ultimately Poirier couldn't sustain the pressure from the hardened veteran and fell in a unanimous decision to Swanson.

Poirier recovered and later destroyed Diego Brandao at UFC 168 in late 2013. Riled up before the bout because Brandao threatened to stab him in the neck, Poirier didn't take the intimidation tactics lightly. He backed up his vitriol the following night with his fists, pummeling the Brazilian and landing 44 significant strikes in just under five minutes of action. Four months later, Poirier disposed of Akira Corassani in a thrilling bout that was named Fight of the Night, with Poirier landing an early uppercut in the second round to finish it.

With Jose Aldo abdicating the featherweight throne to fight at 155 pounds, Poirier will be looking to rise into the top 5 as the division opens up (by 2014, he was the 6th-ranked featherweight). He's openly canvassed for a rematch with Swanson, claiming the first fight was contested under extenuating circumstances. Following the Brandao bout he said, "I took the [Swanson] fight on short notice, cut 30 pounds in a week, flew to London and never felt the feeling I had that night." Poirier has admittedly seen his weight rise to 180 pounds in between scraps, so staying in shape is paramount if he wants to keep fighting at 145 pounds.

The future seems limitless for the Diamond. He may be several fights away from taking a crack at the featherweight belt — caught in the middle between being good but not yet great — but Poirier's still young. The pressure to get here is over; he's no longer a diamond in the rough. Quite the opposite: he's a star.

TALE OF THE TAPE

BORN

UNITED STATES

D.O.B.
1989/01/19

HEIGHT
5'9"

WEIGHT
145 lb.

ASSOCIATION
American Top Team

NICKNAME
The Diamond

CHARLES "MASK" LEWIS

Above: Khabib Nurmagomedov slams Abel Trujillo in their cathweight bout at UFC 160. Nurmagomedov was awarded the unanimous-decision victory. Right: Nurmagomedov scores another unanimous-decision victory, this time over Pat Healy at UFC 165.

IN THE SMALL republic of Dagestan, situated in the Northern Caucasus Mountains alongside the Caspian Sea in the southernmost part of the country, a fighter was born. It was 1988, during the waning years of the Soviet empire. And it was here, in this multilingual, ethnically diverse region prone to violence, that Khabib "the Eagle" Nurmagomedov cut his teeth, emerging from the shadow of the mountains as one of the world's next great mixed martial artists.

He's never lost a fight. Let that sink in. Since 2008, the lightweight has fought 22 times.

Twenty-two times the referee has raised his fist in glory. Twenty-two times Nurmagomedov has bested another man in combat. No wonder all eyes have turned to the dangerous Dagestani fighter as a top contender at 155 pounds.

Trained by his father, himself both a wrestler and sambo master, Nurmagomedov was born into a fighting family. (There is even a 20-second video of a nine-year-old Nurmagomedov wrestling a baby bear cub.) Adding a black belt in judo to his toolbox, Nurmagomedov brings to the octagon a multifaceted arsenal of skills that few possess — plus a furry white traditional Dagestani hat that's impossible to miss.

Hip-tossing opponents at will, the 155-pounder uses judo to set up an impressive ground game that's led to seven professional submission victories. Equally comfortable standing up, the 25-year-old has the same number of professional knockouts, including a ruthless first-round stoppage of veteran Thiago Tavares in early 2013 at UFC on FX: Belfort vs. Bisping, where, in top position, he rained down elbows on Tavares' head until the referee called a stop to the bout.

His skill set is difficult to defend against. Versus Abel Trujillo, Nurmagomedov set a UFC record with 21 takedowns in 27 attempts in just one fight. His takedown defense in the UFC is equally impressive at 83 percent, thanks in part to his strong wrestling acumen. And Nurmagomedov is a two-time World Combat sambo champion (sambo is a hybrid sport incorporating elements of judo, MMA and wrestling; Russian MMA legend Fedor Emelianenko was a four-time world champ). Simply, Nurmagomedov finishes fights, giving him added value in a mixed martial arts landscape now dependent on flash and splash from relative unknowns for big ratings.

The lightweight still has a long road ahead to prove he belongs among the elite. He disposed of Trujillo at UFC 160 in 2013 but missed weight prior to the bout, coughing up 20 percent of his purse. He also let his emotions get the better of him during the weigh-in, shoving Trujillo as they posed for the weigh-in photo. The UFC loves a heated press event, but he'll have to manage better if he wants to be considered among the best. UFC president Dana White acknowledged that Nurmagomedov needs to fight high-caliber fighters. Someone, perhaps, like current lightweight champ Anthony Pettis. It seems the two are on a collision course after the Dagestani's most recent win in April 2014, a top-to-bottom domination of Rafael dos Anjos at UFC on Fox 11. If he misses weight again, though, Nurmagomedov won't receive

the same get-out-of-jail-free card — going forward, the lightweight will need to ensure he stays on top of his game with his training regimen and weight cutting.

So is he the next Emelianenko? Possibly. At 22-0 and possessing immeasurable raw talent, a slew of skills and indomitable spirit to win, the young fighter is just getting started and very well might have the potential to be the next great Russian in MMA. He's not the only one seeking that title, however. The golden age for Dagestani/Chechen fighters is happening now, with Rustam Khabilov, Azamat Gashimov and Omari Akhmedov all competing at the UFC level, and a host of others waiting in the wings and fighting in Bellator and M-1.

The all-elusive title shot that fighters seek is what will define Nurmagomedov's career. International mixed martial artists often need several warmup fights when transitioning to the UFC, and Nurmagomedov is no exception — wins are wins, but beating tough competition speaks volumes. He's now training in the United States out of the American Kickboxing Academy in San Jose, California, the same gym as current heavyweight titleholder Cain Velasquez. The new arrangement means he'll be learning from and sparring with top-quality partners. His decision to make the switch to train in America speaks volumes of his will to become a future champion. That doesn't mean he's forgotten where he comes from — suffice it to say that Dagestani hat will be bobbing to the ring for a while yet.

TALE OF THE TAPE

BORN

RUSSIA

D.O.B.
1988/09/20

HEIGHT
5'10"

WEIGHT
155 lb.

ASSOCIATION
Red Fury
Fight Team

NICKNAME
The Eagle

JOHN HATHAWAY

Above: Eventual victor John Hathaway throws his knee into the body of Kris McCray at UFC Fight Night 24. Right: Hathaway unloads on Pascal Krauss at UFC on Fox 3 for his 16th professional victory.

JOHN HATHAWAY MAY be one of the most underrated fighters in the UFC today. The scrappy British welterweight has compiled a professional record of 17-2, with seven of those wins coming in the UFC since he debuted with the organization in 2009. With big British names in MMA at a premium — beyond Michael Bisping and Dan Hardy, the list isn't long — perhaps Hathaway hasn't received enough respect because he doesn't have a very long resume. But since headlining his first card and getting his health in order, that's about to change.

Nicknamed "the Hitman," Hathaway was tracking to be a star in another sport before his UFC career: rugby. His mug showcases an off-kilter nose thanks to the Brighton native's playing days at Shoreham College in Sussex. He transitioned to MMA late in his teens, and by 22, the London Shootfighters member was calling himself a UFC fighter. If there was ever any doubt the young UK welterweight wasn't ready for the big time, his first bout signaled his arrival with a bang: he destroyed veteran Irishman Tom Egan with vicious elbows at UFC 93 in Dublin. Hathaway followed up the win later that year with a unanimous victory over Rick Story — a strong scrapper who owns notable wins over Jake Ellenberger and Johny Hendricks.

Hathaway, however, developed a nasty habit of going the distance, a pattern most fighters seek to avoid, as few want the bout to go to the judges for decision — most would rather shoot for a KO and control their own destiny. Luckily, the 26-year-old has been on the right side of the scorecard almost every time thanks to well-rounded wrestling skills, efficient standup and the ability to ground and pound when the fight heads to the mat. He slipped up, however, versus crafty vet Mike Pyle, a perennial gatekeeper in the welterweight division who managed to surprise the young fighter and hand Hathaway his first loss.

That bout has become a before/after picture of the rising prospect. Prior to Pyle, Hathaway was on a meteoric rise. The Brit demolished well-respected and uber-talented Diego Sanchez at UFC 114 in Las Vegas, and a collective oohing and aahing surrounded the 6-foot-2, 170-pound Brit after he reeled off a four-fight winning streak to begin his UFC career. But the balloon popped after the defeat to Pyle. Hathaway was subsequently devastated when he was diagnosed with ulcerative colitis (or Crohn's disease), and he spent 14 months on the sidelines dealing with his condition. He fought only once in 2011 and was absent for all of 2013, struggling with weight loss, fatigue, stomach cramps and intestinal issues. But with medication, dedication to a new training regimen and an altered diet, the feisty Brit returned the following year, proving to all the doctors who suggested he quit that he was, in the truest sense, a fighter. However, waiting for him upon his return was no slouch: "the Stun Gun."

The scrap with Dong Hyun Kim was a fight in the making for some time, originally slated for UFC 120 in 2010. The Korean welterweight pulled out because of injury, but four years later, they finally touched off in Macao, headlining *The Ultimate Fighter: China* finale at the Cotai Arena, where boxer Manny

Pacquiao fought Brandon Rios in 2013. It was Hathaway's first headline bout and first five-rounder. His height and 75.5-inch reach are usually an issue for opponents in his weight class, but Kim is almost identical in size, presenting an intriguing matchup of similar body types. Hathaway employed strong standup throughout the bout, issuing brutal knees to Kim's body. But the Korean did damage of his own, and even though Hathaway displayed a granite chin for the first two rounds (even Dana White tweeted how impressed he was with the Brighton native), Hathaway ate a spinning elbow flush in the third that knocked out the British fighter and signaled victory for the Korean.

There's still plenty of upside for Hathaway as he begins the long road to recovery. He believes he can fight until 40 years old if he can stay healthy. Possessing a well-rounded set of fighting tools, he'll need to string together a series of wins to one day convince the UFC brass he's worthy of a title shot in a jammed division chock-full of hungry contenders. In the meantime, whether it be a broken nose playing rugby, a debilitating disease or a stiff elbow to the face, it seems the welterweight from the south coast of England is hearty enough that he should be stepping into the octagon for a long, long time.

TALE OF THE TAPE

BORN

🏴󠁧󠁢󠁥󠁮󠁧󠁿

ENGLAND

D.O.B.
1987/07/01

HEIGHT
6'2"

WEIGHT
170 lb.

ASSOCIATION
London
Shootfighters

NICKNAME
The Hitman

PHIL DAVIS

Above and right: Phil Davis and Brian Stann battle at UFC 109. Davis was awarded the unanimous decision for his fifth straight win.

PHIL DAVIS, WHOSE slow ascent up the light heavyweight rankings has him slotted as high as the top 5 for the first time in his career, may perfectly exemplify the epithet "slow and steady wins the race." The MMA star may be pushing 30, but for the man they call "Mr. Wonderful," the ultimate win may be lurking just around the corner.

Born in Harrisburg, Pennsylvania, the 6-foot-2, 205-pounder is a physical specimen. Massive shoulders, ripped abs and powerful legs make the four-time NCAA All-America wrestler difficult to attack, and he ranks top 10 in the UFC in significant strike defense with a 71 percent rating. He has used that wrestling background to his advantage, taking fights to the ground whenever possible and skillfully submitting men at will — 25 percent of his 12 victories have come by submission, including a slick anaconda choke versus then-rising Swedish star (and current training partner) Alexander Gustafsson at UFC 112 in Abu Dhabi in 2010. (The anaconda, similar to a D'Arce choke, is a relatively new jiu-jitsu maneuver credited to Brazilian Milton Vieira just over a decade ago.)

Using a low center of gravity and a long 79-inch reach — Davis averages 2.4 takedowns per fight — the light heavyweight is able to keep challengers at bay, forcing them to make mistakes. Holding a kinesiology degree from Penn State means the American also possesses an understanding of body kinetics that can work to his advantage. Growing up with brothers whom he physically battled for prime seating at the dinner table as well as having a college coach who regularly made him run a mile and a half in under 10 minutes back to back his freshman year has informed his inner fortitude, and all of it has translated to the octagon.

Davis shot out of the gates early on in his MMA career, notching victories versus some seriously tough customers: stand toe to toe with the likes of former military man Brian Stann or the imposing Tim Boetsch, and most men would run. Fear isn't the issue for Davis, though. Finishing fights is. He doesn't knock guys out, and that continues to be a problem for the exceptionally talented fighter — in a world where knockouts remain king, Davis still has an uphill battle if he wants a title shot against reigning champ Jon "Bones" Jones, whom Davis claims he can "break apart like a sugar cookie." However, Jones is three years his junior and arguably the most formidable force the UFC has ever seen. Further, Davis' 2013 decision win versus former light heavyweight champion Lyoto Machida was chastised — many felt Machida did enough to score the win and that Mr. Wonderful didn't push the tempo. Davis' hulking shoulders shrugged off the naysayers after the fight. "I know it was a close fight. I think I definitely did enough." That's MMA though, where a razor's edge defines careers.

Davis is no longer an up-and-coming prospect — he's an established one — so the question remains: can the light heavyweight take the next step and become the number one challenger, or will he remain a perennial top-10 contender? He's already been the marquee name on several big fight nights (a win versus Brazilian Antonio Rodrigo

Nogueira at UFC Fight Night: Nogueira vs. Davis, a loss to fellow American Rashad Evans at UFC on Fox: Evans vs. Davis), but that was several years ago, and he still has a lot to prove, especially after a tough loss versus Anthony "Rumble" Johnson at UFC 172 in April 2014. Riding a four-fight unbeaten streak, a win would have vaulted Davis into title talk, but against the heavy striker with strong takedown defense, the former Penn State wrestler's fists failed to set up any of the single or double legs he shot for throughout the three-round fight. Davis sports just a 35 percent significant strike accuracy per fight and still needs work on his standup game to hold his own against powerful punchers like Johnson.

A rematch with Gustafsson, his good friend at Alliance MMA out of San Diego, isn't out of the question one day if Davis strings together several wins. Or Davis may find himself facing a very tough adversary in current number one contender Glover Teixeira, who carried a 20-fight unbeaten streak before suffering a loss to Jones. If Jones continues cleaning out the light heavyweight division, there's speculation the current 205-pound belt holder could move up to heavyweight and fight an entirely new class of men. For Davis, now 12-2-1, that might just be the most wonderful news of all.

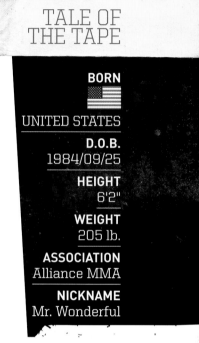

TALE OF THE TAPE

BORN

UNITED STATES

D.O.B.
1984/09/25

HEIGHT
6'2"

WEIGHT
205 lb.

ASSOCIATION
Alliance MMA

NICKNAME
Mr. Wonderful

BEN ASKREN

Above and right: Ben Askren employs some ground and pound to subdue Dan Hornbuckle at the Bellator Fighting Championships 22. The win was Askren's sixth straight.

IT MIGHT BE strange to think of a 29-year-old with 12 professional fights under his belt as just getting started. But Ben Askren is no ordinary mixed martial artist. The Wisconsin-born welterweight may be the best fighter in the world not currently in the UFC.

The wrestling specialist, AKA "Funky," grew up in Hartland, a Milwaukee suburb that's also produced Dallas Cowboys defensive tackle Nick Hayden. Rising to high school state wrestling champion twice, Askren continued to shine at the University of Missouri, winning the NCAA championship in both 2006 and

2007. During his senior year at Mizzou, he compiled a 42-0 win streak in his weight class, finishing with a remarkable lifetime record of 153-8. He holds a laundry list of wrestling awards, including two Dan Hodge collegiate wrestler of the year awards, four All-America selections and an induction to the University of Missouri's Athletic Hall of Fame. But the wrestling standout wasn't satisfied with simple college accolades. He had loftier goals, and putting his money where his mouth was, he qualified for the 2008 Beijing Olympics, competing in the 74 kg division.

Askren disappointingly fell to Cuban wrestler Ivan Fundora, ending his quest for a gold medal at the Summer Olympics. But the following year, the 5-foot-10, 170-pounder made his MMA debut in Columbia, Missouri, dropping Josh Flowers at 1:25 of the first round. Funky hasn't lost since, racking up 12 straight wins and becoming Bellator's welterweight titleholder, a belt he defended four times. His first Bellator bout began impressively when he slipped an anaconda choke around the neck of opponent Ryan Thomas in the first round. They even fought a rematch shortly thereafter, with Askren triumphing once again.

His final bout with the organization was perhaps his most memorable. Facing Andrey Koreshkov in July 2013 at Bellator 97, the lanky, unpredictable Askren didn't just end the bout—he outhit his opponent 248-3 before the referee finally put an end to the Russian's misery in the fourth round. Employing a relentless attack, the welterweight mixed takedowns with vicious ground and pound, finally ending with Askren on Koreshkov's back, wailing punches on the stunned challenger. It was the second straight stoppage for the wrestling-first welterweight, taking him one step closer to altering his image as a one-trick pony.

Never short on hubris, Askren declared after the title bout: "Andrey said he's never been broken. Well, snap, crackle and pop! I'm the best fighter in the world." But after contract negotiations with Bellator CEO Bjorn Rebney went sour, Askren — ranked as high as fifth in the world by Sherdog.com — went seeking greener pastures. But there was a kink in his plan: the outspoken, Afroed mixed martial artist hasn't exactly endeared himself to the UFC in recent years, and president Dana White isn't a fan, claiming Askren is "just not his type of guy." Following UFC 170 in February 2014, the Wisconsin native called out White on Twitter, calling him fat, bald and egotistical and questioning the talent level of the fighters in the co–main event — not exactly the most effective way to land a future job with the premier fight organization in the world.

White just simply isn't interested. After negotiations broke down with the UFC, the 29-year-old quickly signed a two-year, six-fight contract with ONE FC, an Asian fight organization based in Singapore. He's by far the biggest name on the expanding roster and should provide a centerpiece for a growing international fight scene.

It's not always rosy with Askren, and he certainly has his detractors. He's been called one-dimensional and accused of beating up on lesser competition (his closest bout was a narrow victory over veteran Jay Hieron, who once fought Georges St-Pierre in 2004 at UFC 48, but whose UFC record stands at an abysmal 0-4). That hasn't stopped Askren from continuing to do nothing but win, including a first-round submission victory in his debut with ONE FC in May 2014. And if he "runs the table" in ONE FC—as Rebney indicated his former employee would have done in the UFC—it will be only a matter of time before Dana White and co. simply cannot ignore the fighter with so much potential. Plus, a beef with the brass is always good for ticket sales.

Just in case the fight game ends prematurely, Askren's also an accomplished disc golf player, finishing ninth at the U.S. Amateur Disc Golf Championship in 2011, so if the brash fighter is ever looking for a second career, albeit less financially fruitful, he's got a fallback sport. Which is definitely a little bit on the funky side.

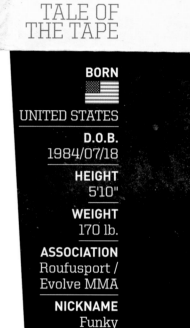

TALE OF THE TAPE

BORN
UNITED STATES

D.O.B.
1984/07/18

HEIGHT
5'10"

WEIGHT
170 lb.

ASSOCIATION
Roufusport /
Evolve MMA

NICKNAME
Funky

GUNNAR NELSON

Above: Gunnar Nelson secures a guillotine choke submission against Omari Akhmedov to win their welterweight fight at UFC Fight Night: Gustafsson vs. Manuwa. Right: Nelson kicks Jorge Santiago in his unanimous decision victory at UFC on Fuel TV 7.

FOR MANY YEARS mixed martial arts was dominated by Brazil, the United States and Japan, but today it has truly become a worldwide sport. That's especially true when considering the success of Gunnar "Gunni" Nelson, who hails from the tiny nation of Iceland, which has less than half a million citizens. Nelson started his athletic career playing hockey and soccer, but after showing an early aptitude for karate, the Icelander switched full time to mastering the ancient Japanese art. He went on to win every karate tournament he entered over a two-year period during his teens. Shifting to grappling, the black belt karate expert overtook the submission grappling world, winning global jiu-jitsu events and even beating a former UFC heavyweight at the 2009 Abu Dhabi Combat Club Submission Wrestling World Championship.

Since drawing his first professional MMA fight, Nelson, whose grandfather was American — hence the very un-Icelandic surname — has ripped off win after win, establishing himself as one of the upcoming welterweight prospects on the UFC circuit. If the soft-spoken Icelander keeps climbing the ladder, it won't be long before we see this tough-as-nails jiu-jitsu master standing in the center of a Las Vegas ring.

His family is pretty tough, too. His father, Haraldur Dean Nelson, is also his coach. An uncle serves in the U.S. Marine Corps. His sister Maria's middle name is Dogg. He's trained with the Gracies and BJ Penn, so clearly the legends of the sport see a lot of potential in the young fighter. At 5-foot-11, 170 pounds and possessing a 72-inch reach, the blond-haired, goateed grappler trains internationally: in Reykjavik with Mjolnir, where his photos are everywhere; in New York with the legendary Renzo Gracie, who awarded Nelson a black belt in Brazilian jiu-jitsu in 2009; and in Ireland with coach John Kavanagh and alongside featherweight phenom Conor McGregor.

Suffice it to say, opponents had better not let the European prospect take the fight to the ground, lest they be submitted. Just ask DaMarques Johnson, whom the 25-year-old choked out in the first round of their catch-weight bout in Nottingham, England, in 2012 at UFC on Fuel TV 5 — Nelson's UFC debut. Opening with a head kick, Nelson took Johnson to the mat and executed his game plan to perfection, pulling mount, wrapping a figure-four leg lock around Johnson's body and sinking a rear naked choke for the win at just 3:34 of the opening round. Nelson said following his debut: "The fight went great, pretty much as good as it could have been. I'm really happy to be here."

His self-defense-first style mimics that of another UFC karate expert, Brazilian Lyoto Machida, the former light heavyweight champion. He also possesses a wide, bouncy stance that often switches back and forth between orthodox and southpaw, low hands and a mixture of unconventional kicks mixed with top-level jiu-jitsu. This skill set was in full effect during Nelson's second UFC scrap against Jorge Santiago at UFC on Fuel TV 7. The bout went the distance, and it was only the second time Nelson has needed to rely on extensive cardio training to pick up the W. Securing two takedowns and connecting with 53 percent of his significant strikes in the unanimous win

versus the veteran, Nelson put his ground and pound on full display, but it was also clear he still needs work on his striking and standup game.

On March 8, 2014, versus Omari Akhmedov at UFC Fight Night 37 in London, England, he barely needed to remain standing. Despite a 13-month layoff due to injury, Nelson appeared fresh and ready. After absorbing several early kicks from his opponent, the welterweight stayed patient and calm, catching the Dagestani fighter with an uppercut and shooting for a takedown. Once on the ground, he went to work like one of the best in the business, positioning himself in full mount and pressing the action with elbows to the head. When Akhmedov tried to escape, the Icelander simply rolled with him and sunk a perfect guillotine choke to end the fight at 4:36 of the opening round. Even his training partner, Irish featherweight Conor McGregor, gave the submission a standing ovation.

Nelson has finished 10 fights in the first round. The Icelandic grappler is a classically trained BJJ prodigy averaging nearly two submissions per bout. Time will tell if he can trade blows with the bad boys — the welterweight division is notoriously tough and populated with hard punchers like Johny Hendricks and Robbie Lawler. Will a submission artist like Gunni make room for himself in the top 10? With a high fighting IQ and, thus far, near-perfect execution, absolutely.

TALE OF THE TAPE

BORN
ICELAND

D.O.B.
1988/07/28

HEIGHT
5'11"

WEIGHT
170 lb.

ASSOCIATION
Mjolnir / SBG
Ireland

NICKNAME
Gunni

CONOR McGREGOR

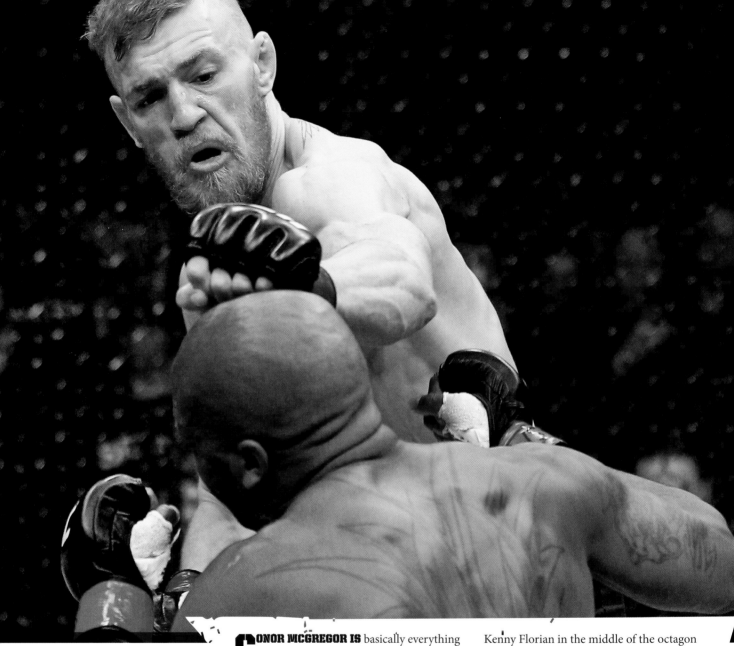

Above: Conor McGregor connects with Marcus Brimage's face in their featherweight fight at UFC on Fuel TV 9, a TKO victory for McGregor. Right: McGregor mounts Max Holloway to help secure victory at UFC Fight Night: Shogun vs. Sonnen.

CONOR McGREGOR IS basically everything you want in an unknown commodity looking to make a name for himself on the world stage. The fast-talking, faux-hawked featherweight is capable of scoring wins in bunches, and he's only getting better. He's brash. He's loud. He's Irish. He's "Notorious" Conor McGregor.

In his UFC debut, McGregor made quite an impression, scoring Knockout of the Night on Apr 6, 2013, in Stockholm versus Marcus Brimage, a first-round KO. After the bout, McGregor was all smiles, standing with Kenny Florian in the middle of the octagon and yelling "60 G's baby! Ha ha!" into the microphone, referencing his bonus money. For the former plumber — who'd collected a welfare check a week before the fight in Sweden — it was the beginning of a lifelong dream to compete at the highest level.

McGregor's path to the UFC started by training early on with the first Irish fighter in the promotion, Tom Egan, and under John Kavanagh, the same coach of rising welterweight star Gunnar Nelson. In 2011, he knocked out some plug named Paddy

Doherty in three-and-a-half seconds, the second-fastest KO in MMA history. (The quickest knockout in the UFC belongs to Duane Ludwig, who put Jonathan Goulet to sleep at six seconds of the first round in their 2006 matchup at UFC Fight Night 3.) McGregor's last bout in 2012 before getting the call to join the UFC was a devastating show of skill and force. Taking on Ivan Buchinger, the Irishman backed him up with an early sweeping kick and then plowed into his opponent, taking him to the ground, revealing a well-rounded set of skills to go along with his hard hands. The two eventually got back up, but it wasn't long before Buchinger was back on the mat courtesy of a stiff left. He never recovered, and the impressive KO stopped the fight at 3:40 of the first round. By spring the following year, the featherweight was doing the same thing to Brimage in the UFC.

The bearded brawler is simply a force to be reckoned with. He cuts an imposing figure at 145 pounds — lithe, muscular and ferocious on his feet, he's a fighter with a multitude of skills: excellent boxing, a purple belt in Brazilian jiu-jitsu and a capoeira-style kicking motion that's difficult to predict. The tattooed featherweight's career 14-2, and he's finished 10 opponents in the opening round alone. But McGregor can also go the distance, as he proved in the summer of 2013 after a unanimous three-round win versus Max Holloway at UFC Fight Night 26 in Boston. McGregor's pace was outstanding. He controlled the fight early and often, both standing up and on the ground — his adrenaline more than likely boosted by the Irish-partisan crowd. But he blew out his ACL during the bout and has since been recovering, leaving everyone to wait and see what the promising featherweight will accomplish when he's healthy. McGregor's war of words in late 2013 with division stalwart Diego Sanchez — he called his fellow featherweight a "has-been . . . [who] should be in Bellator with all the other has-beens" — has all the makings of a legendary fight down the road.

For the Irishman's fans, there is *The Rise of Conor McGregor*, a documentary filmed during his preparation for the Holloway bout — his first on American soil. The film is a fascinating behind-the-scenes peek of the larger-than-life personality — the 25-year-old is a sunglasses-wearing, potty-mouthed, fast-car kind of a guy who is fiercely patriotic and enormously dedicated to training. So bet large that McGregor — whom Dana White has called "a beast" — returns to the UFC at 100 percent and even hungrier than before to prove he's the top dog at 145 pounds.

With the UFC set to land in Dublin during the summer of 2014, their second venture into Ireland, expect Notorious to feature prominently. With Jose Aldo moving up to featherweight, the division is a hotbed of intrigue. And with European events on the rise (Berlin and Istanbul have been added to the ever-growing world domination of the UFC), a star from across the pond is exactly what the UFC could use in selling tickets beyond North America and Brazil. In a press conference prior to the Holloway fight, McGregor said, "Two things I like to do is whoop ass and look good." Forget wins or losses — if he stays true to his words, he'll remain undefeated.

TALE OF THE TAPE

BORN

IRELAND

D.O.B.
1988/07/14

HEIGHT
5'8"

WEIGHT
145 lb.

ASSOCIATION
SBG Ireland

NICKNAME
Notorious

STEFAN STRUVE

Above: Stefan Struve pounds Dave Herman at UFC on Fuel TV 1 for a TKO punches victory. Right: Struve tries to choke out Christian Morecraft at UFC 117. He eventually won via knockout.

SUPERMAN WAS KNOWN to leap over tall buildings in a single bound, but "the Man of Steel" never met "Skyscraper" Stefan Struve, the 7-foot Dutch heavyweight who towers over every other fighter he's ever faced. He may be massive but he's far from invincible. One of the brightest stars in a division laden with talent, Struve will need to mount a comeback of monumental proportions to reestablish his status as a top contender.

Lest he be judged by size alone, Struve developed an early affinity for jiu-jitsu in the Netherlands after he and his brother decided on a whim to go to an MMA gym. With an unorthodox frame and exceptional ability to work from the ground, Struve earned a litany of submission victories early in his career. You name it, he did it. From triangle chokes to rear naked chokes to armbars, Struve showcased a vast array of bodywork that left opponents in Europe wondering: where did this giant come from?

That same thought entered the minds of fans in London, England, on the evening of February 21, 2009, when all 7 feet and 238 pounds of Struve strode into the ring. He didn't last long. Facing another rising star (and future heavyweight champion), Junior dos Santos, Struve didn't make it past the first minute with the dangerous Brazilian boxer. His kryptonite was exposed: hard-punching strikers who close the distance of his ridiculous 84.5-inch reach (tied for longest in the UFC with Jon "Bones" Jones). But drawing on his experience fighting in Europe at a young age, the Dutchman rattled off a three-fight winning streak in the UFC following the dos Santos loss. Two of those wins were by submission, firmly establishing him as one of the best ground talents in the big-boy division. Then — seemingly unsatisfied with being labeled a one-trick pony — Struve laid to rest the notion he couldn't finish opponents, dropping divisional stalwarts Dave Herman and Stipe Miocic with knockout victories. The Miocic victory was particularly impressive. Utilizing a strong jab and high kicks to keep the distance, Struve swarmed the American-Croatian in the second round, earning a stoppage and delivering Miocic his first and only professional loss.

Skyscraper has had his fair share of defeats, too. But his UFC losses have come at the hands of some household names in the heavyweight division: impossible-to-miss bearded brawler Roy Nelson, top-5 contender Travis Browne and fan favorite Mark Hunt. The loss to Hunt was decisive, as the Maori striker delivered a knockout blow to Struve's chin in round three of their fight at UFC on Fuel TV: Stann vs. Silva in March 2013. The punch was so powerful it broke the Dutchman's jaw — the X-ray of which he later shared with his fans on twitter. While admirable that Struve would choose to stand with the mighty Maori known for his lead fists and granite chin, the Dutchman's improved striking skills are not yet up to speed with the top heavyweights.

Struve vowed to come back stronger after the knockout. But just months later he was dealt another sudden blow. This time it wasn't his jaw. It was his heart: it was enlarged, something called "sport heart," common to professional athletes but serious enough to

shut him down. He underwent extensive testing, and it was discovered that Struve also had a leaky bicuspid aortic valve, a congenital heart condition that causes blood to slowly pump back into the heart. At the time, Dana White didn't think the heavyweight would ever fight again. But, in the months since the diagnosis, Struve's condition has greatly improved. As he told The MMA Hour in January 2014, "Don't worry, I'm coming back." Struve was slated to fight at UFC 175 in July, but suffered, "a non-life-threatening, near-fainting spell backstage," said the UFC said in a statement. He was removed from the card for precaution, and White told the media that Struve had passed out while warming up and that doctors initially thought it might be a panic attack. The setback was disappointing for the big fighter; the hope is that it was just another hurdle on the road to returning to the octagon.

Fighting professionally since 2005, the 26-year-old has already amassed a 25-6 record. Prior to the Hunt loss, he'd finished his last four fights either by knockout or submission. But Struve's career is still very much in jeopardy. He's a fighter, that's for sure, all 7 feet of him, and if anybody can come back from something like this, it's Struve. What a tall tale it would be if the man they call Skyscraper could return from such adversity and one day capture the heavyweight belt.

TALE OF THE TAPE

BORN

NETHERLANDS

D.O.B.
1988/02/18

HEIGHT
7'0"

WEIGHT
238 lb.

ASSOCIATION
Team Schrijber

NICKNAME
Skyscraper

ANTHONY PETTIS

Above: Anthony Pettis uncorks a flying head kick on Benson Henderson to help secure victory at World Extreme Cagefighting 53 – the last WEC event ever held. Right: Pettis again connects his foot to Henderson's head, this time at UFC 164 in 2013, which he won to take the UFC lightweight title.

GOOGLE "ANTHONY PETTIS head kick" and you'll see a 23-second clip viewed over five million times. It's a fantastic display of athleticism. The fight in question is Pettis' final fight in the World Extreme Cagefighting circuit before he made the leap to the UFC — and leap is exactly what Pettis does here: Taking two steps to run to the wall, Pettis jumps and plants his right foot halfway up the cage. He then loads his weight against the cage and propels himself off the wall while simultaneously firing a superkick with the same foot! His kick connects with Benson

Henderson's chin, dropping him to the mat. The announcers could barely contain themselves, with one exclaiming: "He ran off the wall like a ninja! I've never seen anything like that." The announcer wasn't the only one. The fight ended with Pettis winning the WEC lightweight championship, vaulting him into the UFC's limelight, where "Showtime" hasn't disappointed since arriving.

It wasn't the first time the 27-year-old had dropped someone with a kick to the head. In just his third professional fight, Pettis was facing a grappler. Taken down early and hard by Mike Lambrecht, Pettis knew he'd dislocated his shoulder immediately. Less than two minutes into the first round, it appeared the lightweight would suffer his first loss. But instead of tapping out, Pettis, to the amazement of his corner, got back up and with one swift motion, he demolished the older fighter with a kick to the head, knocking him out cold.

In the first five fights of his career, Pettis had five first-round victories. That's how you earn a nickname like Showtime. And that's how Anthony Pettis established himself in Milwaukee, Wisconsin, as one of the baddest men at 155 pounds.

Well-honed taekwondo skills in high school have transferred well to mixed martial arts for Pettis. Growing up in a gritty Milwaukee neighborhood, the youngster constantly had to prove himself, especially after the sudden death of his father in a botched robbery at a family friend's home when Pettis was just 15 years old. Anthony drifted for several years afterward, but he eventually found MMA and a changed life. Winning didn't hurt, either. In 2010, Pettis manhandled the WEC's lightweight division, winning four fights in one calendar year, culminating in the title win.

Fast-forward four years and the lightning-quick fighter has risen to the top of the UFC's 155-pound weight class, defeating — guess who? — his old foe Benson Henderson at UFC 164 in 2013. His armbar submission versus "Bendo" for the belt wasn't typical highlight-reel material, unlike his previous fights against perennial tough customers Donald Cerrone and Joe Lauzon. Both succumbed to Pettis' devastating quickness, and neither of them escaped the first round. Cerrone ate a liver shot that buckled the normally fierce fighter. Lauzon didn't even see the head kick coming — in a flash he was on his back, succumbing to a flurry of fight-ending punches. Moral of the story: Pettis doesn't just beat people anymore — he embarrasses them.

The one knock against Pettis? Injuries have been commonplace for the Wisconsin native, and he needed a full year off to heal two labrum tears in his shoulder. He hurt

both knees in 2013 on two separate occasions, which means plans to defend his newly acquired belt are on hold. All signs point to a planned superfight with current featherweight champ Jose Aldo, who is planning to vacate his belt and move up a weight class after defending his title six times at 145 pounds. "Of course I want that fight. Why wouldn't I?" Pettis said in February 2014. But it will have to wait: Pettis has agreed to coach opposite number one contender Gilbert Melendez on *The Ultimate Fighter 20*, culminating in a title fight between the two men at the end of 2014.

Fight fans itching for more Pettis can always turn to the bantamweights. Sergio, Anthony's younger brother, has recently signed with the UFC and seems to possess the same explosive potential as his older sibling. He'll have a lot to live up to, however. Anthony is just 27, still several years away from his prime fighting years. He's already racked up a 17-2 record and owns two Knockout of the Night awards and one Submission of the Night at the UFC level. At 5-foot-9, Anthony is not physically imposing, but his lethal ability to knock men off their feet has made him a must-see attraction.

The reign of former longtime lightweight champ Frankie Edgar is a distant memory. It's Pettis' time now. Showtime.

TALE OF THE TAPE

BORN

UNITED STATES

D.O.B.
1987/01/27

HEIGHT
5'9"

WEIGHT
155 lb.

ASSOCIATION
Roufusport

NICKNAME
Showtime

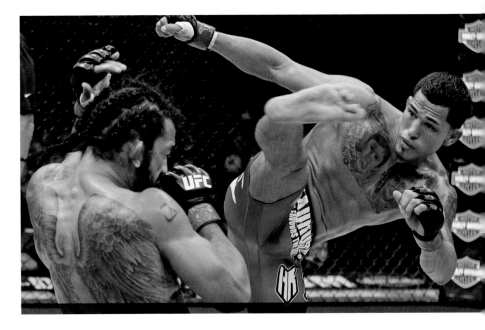

UFC CHAMPION LIST

HEAVYWEIGHT CHAMPIONS

MARK COLEMAN
UFC 12: February 7, 1997
Defenses: 0

MAURICE SMITH
UFC 14: July 27, 1997
Defenses: 1

RANDY COUTURE
UFC Japan: December 21, 1997
Defenses: 0

BAS RUTTEN
(defeated Kevin Randleman
for vacant title)
UFC 20: May 7, 1999
Defenses: 0

KEVIN RANDLEMAN
(defeated Pete Williams for
vacant title)
UFC 23: November 19, 1999
Defenses: 1

RANDY COUTURE
UFC 28: November 17, 2000
Defenses: 2

JOSH BARNETT
UFC 36: March 22, 2002
Defenses: 0

RICCO RODRIGUEZ
(defeated Randy Couture for
vacant title)
UFC 39: September 27, 2002
Defenses: 0

TIM SYLVIA
UFC 41: February 28, 2003
Defenses: 1

FRANK MIR
(defeated Tim Sylvia for
vacant title)
UFC 48: June 19, 2004
Defenses: 0

ANDREI ARLOVSKI
(promoted to undisputed
champion after holding
interim title)
August 12, 2005
Defenses: 1

TIM SYLVIA
UFC 59: April 15, 2006
Defenses: 2

RANDY COUTURE
UFC 68: March 3, 2007
Defenses: 1

BROCK LESNAR
(defeated Randy Couture for
vacant title)
UFC 91: November 15, 2008
Defenses: 2

CAIN VELASQUEZ
UFC 121: July 3, 2010
Defenses: 0

JUNIOR DOS SANTOS
UFC on Fox 1: November 12,
2011. Defenses: 0

CAIN VELASQUEZ
UFC 155: December 29, 2012
Defenses: 2

LIGHT HEAVYWEIGHT CHAMPIONS

FRANK SHAMROCK
UFC Japan: December 21, 1997
Defenses: 4

TITO ORTIZ
(defeated Wanderlei Silva for
vacant title)
UFC 25: April 14, 2000
Defenses: 5

RANDY COUTURE
(defeated Tito Ortiz for
vacant title)
UFC 44: September 26, 2003
Defenses: 0

VITOR BELFORT
UFC 46: January 31, 2004
Defenses: 0

RANDY COUTURE
UFC 49: August 21, 2004
Defenses: 0

CHUCK LIDDELL
UFC 52: April 16, 2005
Defenses: 4

QUINTON JACKSON
UFC 71: May 26, 2007
Defenses: 1

FORREST GRIFFIN
UFC 86: July 5, 2008
Defenses: 0

RASHAD EVANS
UFC 92: December 27, 2008
Defenses: 0

LYOTO MACHIDA
UFC 98: May 23, 2009
Defenses: 1

MAURICIO RUA
UFC 113: May 8, 2010
Defenses: 0

JON JONES
UFC 128: March 19, 2011
Defenses: 7

MIDDLEWEIGHT CHAMPIONS

DAVE MENNE
UFC 33: September 28, 2001
Defenses: 0

MURILO BUSTAMANTE
UFC 35: January 11, 2002
Defenses: 1

EVAN TANNER
(defeated David Terrell for
vacant title)
UFC 51: February 5, 2005
Defenses: 0

RICH FRANKLIN
UFC 53: June 4, 2005
Defenses: 2

ANDERSON SILVA
UFC 64: October 14, 2006
Defenses: 10

CHRIS WEIDMAN
UFC 162: July 6, 2013
Defenses: 2

WELTERWEIGHT CHAMPIONS

PAT MILETICH
UFC Brazil: October 16, 1998
Defenses: 4

CARLOS NEWTON
UFC 31: May 4, 2001
Defenses: 0

MATT HUGHES
UFC 34: November 2, 2001
Defenses: 5

BJ PENN
UFC 46: January 31, 2004
Defenses: 0

MATT HUGHES
(defeated Georges St-Pierre
for vacant title)
UFC 50: October 22, 2004
Defenses: 2

GEORGES ST-PIERRE
UFC 65: November 18, 2006
Defenses: 0

MATT SERRA
UFC 69: April 7, 2007
Defenses: 0

GEORGES ST-PIERRE
(defeated Matt Serra for
vacant title)
UFC 83: April 19, 2008
Defenses: 9

JOHNY HENDRICKS
(defeated Robbie Lawler for
vacant title)
UFC 171: March 15, 2014
Defenses: 0

LIGHTWEIGHT CHAMPIONS

JENS PULVER
UFC 30: February 23, 2001
Defenses: 2

SEAN SHERK
(defeated Kenny Florian for
vacant title)
UFC 64: October 14, 2006
Defenses: 1

BJ PENN
(defeated Joe Stevenson for
vacant title)
UFC 80: January 19, 2008
Defenses: 3

FRANKIE EDGAR
UFC 112: April 10, 2010
Defenses: 1

BENSON HENDERSON
UFC 144: February 26, 2012
Defenses: 3

ANTHONY PETTIS
UFC 164: August 31, 2013
Defenses: 0

The UFC championship belt: the most prestigious prize in MMA. Below: Tito Ortiz wraps the light heavyweight belt around the waist of Randy Couture at UFC 44 after being dismissed by unanimous decision in their five-round match. Couture failed to defend the title, losing it to Vitor Belfort four months later.

FEATHERWEIGHT CHAMPIONS

JOSE ALDO
UFC 123: November 20, 2010
Defenses: 6

BANTAMWEIGHT CHAMPIONS

DOMINICK CRUZ
(defeated Scott Jorgensen for WEC/UFC unification title)
WEC 53: December 16, 2010
Defenses: 2

RENAN BARAO
(promoted to undisputed champion after holding interim title)
January 6, 2014
Defenses: 1

T.J. DILLASHAW
UFC 173: May 24, 2014
Defenses: 0

FLYWEIGHT CHAMPIONS

DEMETRIOUS JOHNSON
UFC 152: September 22, 2012
Defenses: 4

WOMEN'S BANTAMWEIGHT CHAMPIONS

RONDA ROUSEY
(promoted to undisputed champion after holding Strikeforce title)
December 6, 2012
Defenses: 4

ACKNOWLEDGMENTS

I ATTENDED UFC 19 in March of 1999 fully planning to do an exposé on what I had assumed was nothing more than human cockfighting. Boy, was I wrong. I met many fighters, managers, media members and executives involved with the sparsely attended event, and after the three-day affair I left with an entirely different opinion and plan. Ken Shamrock, Guy Mezger, Monte Cox, Pat Miletich, Jeremy Horn, Kevin Randleman, "Big" John McCarthy and the late Jeff Blatnick were generous with their time, knowledge and passion for the sport, and they quickly helped me understand that mixed martial arts, if presented correctly, would be massively popular.

On that trip I also became friends with *Full Contact Fighter* founder Joel Gold (who has some pictures in this book) and fighter Gary Goodridge, and both men have been very helpful over the years. Joel and I later started *Full Contact Fighter TV*, the first ever nationally broadcast weekly MMA television show. Lorenzo Fertitta and Dana White generously supported us, and I'd like to thank them for their help; more importantly, though, I'd like to salute their vision and willingness to invest a great deal of time and money to make MMA into the mainstream sport it has become today.

Most importantly I'd like to thank my editor, Steve Cameron. In a very busy year for him personally, he provided immense amounts of patience, understanding and support, all of which made it possible for me to contribute to the making of this book. Thanks Steve!

– Brian Sobie

BOOKS ARE VERY much collaborative efforts, so I'd like to first thank my editor, Steve Cameron, whose guiding hand in putting together *MMA Now!* has been immeasurable. I'd also like to extend thanks to publisher Lionel Koffler, designer Matt Filion, copyeditor Patricia MacDonald and everyone at Firefly Books who helped make this book a reality. And thank you to my co-author, Brian Sobie: your astute insight, particularly with regard to the early days of MMA, was a huge help.

I'd like to acknowledge the UFC, and in particular UFC Canada, whose professionalism and assistance in securing interviews and granting access over the last several years has been nothing less than first class. And a thank you to the talented team at *Sportsnet* magazine who worked with me on a variety of MMA stories over the years.

I'd also like to thank my parents, David and Esther Segal, and my sister, Michelle, for their unwavering support throughout my career.

Fight fans are a special breed. I've enjoyed talking shop with diehard fans at my local bar or friends at my regular fight night. But there are two longtime MMA friends, Joris and Adam, who deserve a special nod. I've watched every big fight in recent memory with those two, and they have patiently answered every question I've had — they have also tolerated my unabashed love for Nick Diaz.

It is their passion for combat sports that has inspired me from the beginning. Thank you.

– Adam Elliott Segal

PHOTO CREDITS

GETTY IMAGES

Sankei Archive: 14; Al Bello: 52, 57, 68, 73, 117, 121;
Markus Boesch: 16TL; Jeff Bottari: 5, 6, 21, 44, 50 (Weidman),
50 (Aldo), 50 (Dillashaw), 50 (Johnson), 72, 82R; Culture Club: 13;
Henry S. Dziekan III: 110; Jonathan Ferrey: 94; Josh Hedges: 2, 10, 12,
20, 22, 24, 25, 32-43, 46, 47TL, 50 (Petis), 51, 54, 55, 60-62, 64-65, 67,
69-71, 74, 77, 80-81, 83-84, 85, 88-89, 92, 96-103, 109L, 113-116,
118-120, 122-125, 128-134, 137; Kari Hubert: 78; Jed Jacobsohn: 48,
66, 95; Jim Kemper: 50 (Velasquez), 50 (Jones), 50 (Hendricks), 50
(Rousey), 82L, 82C; Jon Kopaloff: 86, 90; Nick Laham: 47BL, 75, 91;
Esther Lin: 63; Brandon Magnus: 109R; Buda Mendes: 111;
Jason Merritt: 19; Ethan Miller: 108; Donald Miralle: 47R, 56, 76, 93;
Ed Mulholland: 135; William R. Sallaz: 16BL; Holly Stein: 16R;
Richard Wolowicz: 104; Zuffa LLC: 8, 17

ADDITIONAL PHOTOGRAPHERS

Joel Gold/fcfighter.com: 26-27
Susumu Nagao: 28-31, 58-59
Dave Mandel: 126-127

FRONT COVER

Jim Kemper/Getty Images: Anderson Silva, Jon Jones,
Georges St-Pierre
Shutterstock/anthonymooney: Arena background

BACK COVER

Josh Hedges/Getty Images

LEGEND

T = Top, TL = Top Left, BL = Bottom Left, R = Right,
L = Left, C = Center

INDEX